FULL SPECTRUM DOMINANCE

FULL SPECTRUM DOMINANCE

U.S. Power in Iraq and Beyond

RAHUL MAHAJAN

AN OPEN MEDIA BOOK

SEVEN STORIES PRESS
NEW YORK

In Canada: Hushion House, 36 Northline Road, Toronto, Ontario M4B 3E2

In the U.K.: Turnaround Publisher Services Ltd., Unit 3, Olympia Trading Estate, Coburg Road, Wood Green, London N22 6TZ

In Australia: Palgrave Macmillan, 627 Chapel Street, South Yarra, VIC 3141

Cover design: Greg Ruggiero
Cover image: March 23, 2003, a U.S. soldier from the 1st Marine Expeditionary Force stands near a burning oil well in Iraq's Rumayla oil fields—the second largest offshore oilfield in the country. IAN WALDIE/GETTY IMAGES

Library of Congress Cataloging-in-Publication Data

Mahajan, Rahul.
  Full spectrum dominance : U.S. power in Iraq and beyond / Rahul Mahajan.-- 1st ed.
    p. cm.
  ISBN 1-58322-578-1 (pbk.)
  1. War on Terrorism, 2001- 2. Sanctions (International law)
3. United States--Foreign relations. 4. Democracy—Iraq. 5. Human rights—Iraq. I. Title: U.S. power in Iraq and beyond. II. Title.
HV6432 .M336 2003
956.7044'3--dc21   2003010279

Printed in Canada.

9 8 7 6 5 4 3 2 1

To the people of Iraq, who have suffered much, in hopes that one day they will achieve a genuine liberation. And to the global antiwar movement, that for one shining moment rocked the halls of power, and will do so again.

I would like to thank Zeynep Tufekci for helping me with this book and for a long and very fruitful political collaboration. Her influence shows up on every page.

Contents

"The overall goal of the transformation described in this document is the creation of a force that is dominant across the full spectrum of military operations—persuasive in peace, decisive in war, preeminent in any form of conflict.

"...Full spectrum dominance—the ability of U.S. forces, operating unilaterally or in combination with multinational and interagency partners, to defeat any adversary and control any situation across the full range of military operations."

—JOINT VISION 2020, released May 30, 2000.

"We don't seek empires. We're not imperialistic. We never have been. I can't imagine why you'd even ask the question."

—DEFENSE SECRETARY DONALD RUMSFELD, when asked by an al-Jazeera correspondent if the Bush administration was bent on "empire-building." Press conference, April 28, 2003.

After the War: U.S. Power in Iraq and Beyond

THE SHORT-TERM POLITICAL calculations of the Bush administration seem to have been borne out. Resolutely ignoring a tidal wave of domestic and international opposition, the administration gambled everything on the idea that "nothing succeeds like success." The genuine joy that the Iraqis felt at the end of Saddam Hussein's extremely brutal rule (and at the foreseen end of the crippling sanctions) has enabled the administration to claim that this was a war of liberation. The comparative restraint with which the war was waged (contrast with, say, the Gulf War, in which electrical power and other necessary civilian infrastructure was systematically bombed, and in which helpless soldiers were slaughtered by the tens of thousands, mercilessly bombed on the "Highway of Death" or buried in the sands of southern Iraq) has led to an outpouring of what can only be called imperialist triumphalism.

Even though thousands of soldiers and civilians were

slaughtered, maimed, and injured by the war, it did not prove difficult to argue that this was a small price to pay for the fact that Iraqis will in many ways be far better off with the end of Hussein and the lifting of U.S.-imposed sanctions. It was easy to forget during this orgy of self-congratulation that the three-week shooting war was simply the culmination of a 13-year war, waged primarily by the United States, against the people of Iraq. The Gulf War and the sanctions likely killed over 1 million people and led to a large-scale breakdown of Iraqi society. It was even easier to forget the fact that Iraq had not used any "weapons of mass destruction" (a term that is applied equally to the very real thermonuclear bombs of the United States and to the hypothesized Iraqi mustard-filled artillery shells)—and that, therefore, the claims that Iraq posed some threat to the United States that had to be "pre-empted" were absurd. If, after all, Saddam Hussein's regime was either unable or unwilling to use the dreaded WMD to save his own rule—the ultimate threat—what would be the circumstances in which he would use them? What possible threat to the world's superpower is posed by a country unable to fly a single plane against an occupying force?

The war was an integral, and perhaps the primary, component in a sweeping new vision of U.S. foreign policy associated with a group of ideologues who call themselves neoconservatives and who have emerged as the dominant influence in this administration. Although the roots of virtually every neoconservative idea can be discerned in the policies of the 1990's, this is the first time in the post–Cold War era that their vision of using direct military means to extend the dominance of the United States has become the central approach.

In particular, the war dramatically increased the United States' long-term capacity for "force projection," not just in the Middle East but, dovetailing with other developments, potentially in the world as well.

U.S. PLANS FOR IRAQ

In a sense, had there been any doubt about U.S. intentions for Iraq, it should have been dispelled when Deputy Defense Secretary Paul Wolfowitz rediscovered the doctrine of "odious debt."

This doctrine was first used in 1898, after the Spanish-American War. The United States had "liberated" Cuba and decided to own it. The most blatant expression of the ownership was the Platt Amendment to the Cuban constitution that gave the United States the right to intervene in Cuba whenever it wished. When Spain pressed for repayment of Cuba's debt to Spain, the United States argued that the debt was invalid because it had been "imposed upon the people of Cuba without their consent and by force of arms."

This basic idea, that debts incurred by an unrepresentative regime need not be repaid by the people, has become part of customary international law and is one of the many arguments that the group Jubilee 2000 used in its largely unsuccessful efforts to get the Third World's foreign debt cancelled. In practice, it is honored more in the breach than the observance. The logic was unexceptionable when Paul Wolfowitz, addressing the Senate Armed Services Committee, said, "I hope...they will think about the very large debts that come from money that was lent to the dictator to buy weapons and to build palaces and to building instruments of repression. I think they ought to consider whether it might not be appropriate to forgive some or all of that debt so the new Iraqi government isn't burdened with it."[1] He did not, however, comment on how this would apply to the debt of the Congo, run up by the kleptocratic U.S.-supported dictator Mobutu Sese Seko, or, even more fitting, to the debt incurred by the apartheid regime of South Africa, long a close strategic ally of the United States.

Things are very different now than they were with Cuba. Almost immediately after "liberating" Iraq, the United States announced its intention to establish four military bases in Iraq, with one official saying, "There will be some kind of a long-term defense relationship with a new Iraq, similar to Afghanistan."[2] Although the report was contested by Defense Secretary Rumsfeld in one of his trademark convoluted semi-denials, the United States has left little doubt that a continued military presence in Iraq is the key component of its plans to transform the Middle East.

OIL

U.S. plans for Iraq's oil are similarly clear. Iraq was the first Arab country to fully nationalize its oil, in 1972. In the 1990's, like other OPEC countries (especially Iran), most of which suffer from the endemic capital short-ages of Third World countries, it began looking to for-eign investment to finance new exploration. Although no agreements could be implemented under the sanc-tions, Iraq signed deals with the oil companies of prac-tically any country that wasn't the United States or the United Kingdom, since they were viewed as the major protagonists of the sanctions—in particular, major exploration agreements were signed with Russian and French companies.

Now, U.S. corporations will have not only an equal chance but a preferred one in any bidding process. Since oil has become a touchy subject for the administration, the preferences will likely not be as blatant as they have been in the initial awarding of reconstruction contracts, where the U.S. government has openly made the deci-sions, foreign corporations were often not invited to bid, and awards often went to companies like Halliburton and Bechtel, closely tied to the military-industrial complex and, in particular, to key figures in both Bush adminis-trations.[3] Still, the war has dramatically improved the chances of U.S. oil companies, to say the least.

There is also talk about denationalizing the wells that

are already producing oil. Thus, Fadhil Chalabi of the State Department's Future of Iraq Oil and Energy Working Group (and cousin of Ahmed Chalabi) advocates "privatization or partial privatization" of the Iraqi state oil companies, a sentiment echoed by other members of the group.[4] Of course, if this occurs, a much smaller percentage of Iraq's oil revenues will then be available to serve the needs of the Iraqi people, since much of the revenue will be siphoned off to profit foreign corporations.

It's interesting to note that the Bush-Cheney energy policy, promulgated in early 2001, calls on the government to continue to use the World Trade Organization Energy Services Negotiations, the Free Trade Area of the Americas, bilateral trade agreements, and similar instruments to "level the playing field for U.S. companies overseas" in the energy sector and to "reduce barriers to trade and investment."[5] How much more straightforward to do it with bombs.

DEMOCRACY

Of course, one might ask how the United States can be so sanguine about these plans for military bases, regional force projection, and increased control of Iraqi oil, given the fact that it is supposedly creating a democracy in Iraq, which might then choose to imperil those plans.

The reason, of course, is that "democracy" is being used as a code word. U.S. intentions are to create a heavily dependent Iraqi government that will not stray far, if at all, from U.S. dictates.

Even before the Pentagon's designated interim ruler of Iraq, Jay Garner, had set foot in the country, it had already become cliché to refer to him as the American proconsul. The fact that in the past Garner publicly praised the "remarkable restraint" of the Israeli Defense Forces certainly showed his own detachment from reality and the Bush administration's blatant disregard for the sensibilities of the Arab public.[6]

Far more important than the identity or sympathies of the proconsul, however, is the fact that a foreign military occupation is not a good breeding ground for democracy or independence. This is all the more so when, as now, the U.S. attitude toward "democracy" has been made so manifest. In the post-9/11 world (and to a large extent before), "democracy" means obedience to U.S. dictates. Thus, Eastern European governments that defied the wishes of their populations to join the latest "coalition of the willing" were praised for their "courage," while Turkey, where the final decision of the government actually accorded with popular opinion, will pay a heavy price, as, say many U.S. government officials, will France.

The creation of "democracy" in Afghanistan demonstrates something of what is to come with Iraq, but Iraq is a more complex case. The necessity to keep Iraq's oil pumping, and even significantly to increase its production, will require a government that has real authority over the whole country; Karzai's writ does not even cover all of Kabul. This may necessitate a slightly broader-based government; certainly, the need to placate and find a role for Iraq's large well-educated middle class will require more of a "free market" economy and less of a kleptocracy.

Still, the basic outlines will be the same, and they had already become visible within days of the war's conclusion. Without even the fake legitimacy of the international meeting in Bonn where other countries signed off on the U.S.-designed process for Afghanistan, the U.S. military convened a series of meetings in Nasiriyah in which selected Iraqi political figures were expected to settle on a process for creating an interim government—without meaningful international or U.N. participation. The Supreme Council for the Islamic Revolution in Iraq, a group that represents some undetermined number of Iraqi Shia, boycotted the meetings—although the group joined some later "invitation only" meetings, it has consistently called for withdrawal of U.S troops. The Iraqi Communist Party, the first political party in Iraqi history that developed a mass base and did mass popular mobilization, was excluded from the meetings by the Americans, as were other groups.[7]

Across the political spectrum, from Adnan Pachachi, former Foreign Minister of the pre-Ba'ath 1968 Iraqi government, to the Communist Party, there were calls for a U.N.-sponsored conference, rather than one held by the U.S. military, so that Iraqis could genuinely exercise their right to decide their destiny.[8]

Many Iraqis, happy to be free of Saddam Hussein, are not happy to see any American presence continue. Within days of the war's end, there was a mass protest of 20,000 in Nasiriyah, in which Iraqis said, "Yes to Freedom, No to America, No to Saddam." Numerous others took place across the country. On separate occasions, at least 13 protesters were killed by U.S. forces in Mosul, 13 in Baghdad, and 15 in Fallujah.[9]

Had the United States wished to create a genuinely democratic process, the way was clear. Maximal consultation and participation is necessary, leading eventually to a constitutional convention, something like the one that created the American constitution. To keep the country stabilized in the meantime, an impartial force would have been necessary—the only option being, of course, a multinational U.N. peacekeeping force.

Instead, with the phenomenal leverage that the United States exerts and will continue to exert through its military presence and the selective use of money, it should come as no surprise to anyone when an Iraqi government emerges that pays more attention to the Bush administration's conception of U.S. strategic interests than it does to the needs of the Iraqi people.

SYRIA AND IRAN

Even before the war had ended, the United States was indicating the ways it would use its enhanced leverage in the region against other enemies, particularly Iran and Syria. In succession, Donald Rumsfeld, Colin Powell, John Bolton, and numerous other government officials issued thinly veiled threats that the war on Iraq should stand as a lesson to them; in particular, that neither country should continue to support terrorists. The primary "terrorist" group that Syria and Iran are supporting is Hezbollah, an organization that plays a legitimate political role in Lebanon and is no longer considered a terrorist organization by the rest of the world; in recent history, it has almost exclusively concentrated its attacks on the portion of the Israeli military that was occupying Lebanon, not on civilian targets. Those efforts actually drove the Israeli military out of Lebanon.

It's an open secret that the neoconservatives in the Bush administration desire "regime change" in Syria and Iran, and quite possibly in other states in the region—and that they are willing to use military force, if necessary, to achieve that. The simple presence of the U.S. military has already made a huge difference—shortly after the war concluded, the United States shut off the Iraqi pipeline to Syria, through which 200,000 barrels per day flowed, enabling Syria to export an extra $1.2 billion worth of oil annually.[10] That presence will also enhance the effect of non-military measures—indeed, the Israeli ambassador to the United States, Daniel Ayalon, has called for regime change in Syria and Iran through a combination of diplomatic isolation, economic sanctions, and "psychological pressure."[11] The U.S. Congress also began consideration of a "Syria Accountability Act" that would give the president the right to impose sanctions on Syria.[12]

Very few, even among the neoconservatives, believe that regime change in Iran by military force will be easy to achieve. But with Iraq taken, the U.S. military has now almost completely surrounded Iran. There are U.S. forces in Turkey, Iraq, the Gulf States, Pakistan, Afghanistan, and Turkmenistan, every state that abuts Iran except for Russia. The United States also exercises effective military control over the Straits of Hormuz, through which most of Iran's oil must travel before it is exported to the world.

THE "ROAD MAP" FOR THE ISRAELI-PALESTINIAN CONFLICT

Even more immediately at hand is the use of U.S. leverage in the resumption of what is usually called the "peace process" between Israel and the Palestinians.

The first Gulf War dramatically increased U.S. power in the region (it is from that war that a permanent land-based U.S. military presence in the region dates) and simultaneously deprived the Palestinians of any external allies. The result was the inauguration of the so-called "Oslo process." Billed as a historic attempt at reconciliation between Israelis and Palestinians, in reality it was an attempt to cement the Israeli occupation of the West Bank. The PLO, having no one to turn to, was forced to negotiate away the internationally recognized rights of the Palestinian table in return for some form of local autonomy on a very small portion of their land. As long as there was no Palestinian popular mobilization (as in the intifada), the Israelis had all the leverage at the bargaining table and the Palestinians none. Essentially, the newly formed Palestinian Authority acted as a client state of Israel, policing and repressing the Palestinian people so that the Israelis could without difficulty double the rate of settlement-building, build a series of Israeli-only bypass roads cutting apart the occupied territories, institute numerous security checkpoints, and basically create so many "facts on the ground" that the occupation would never be reversible without prohibitive upheavals in Israeli society.[13]

In 2000, for various reasons, that process broke down. Since then, the debate in Israeli ruling circles is between a resumption of an Oslo-style apartheid and "transfer," a euphemism for some form of mass expulsion of Palestinians. Transfer, if it is the end goal, is not to be achieved by rounding up Palestinians and shipping them out, but by a process of making Palestinian daily life unlivable. The frequent "closures" had by 2002 amounted to a near-permanent state of siege warfare on the Palestinians, with gruesome results—22 percent of children suffered acute or chronic malnutrition and the number of people fed by the U.N. Relief and Works Agency had increased from 300,000 to 1.1 million.[14] Simultaneously, the occupied territories were cut up into tiny blocks, with such lengthy security checks that Palestinians who had to travel would spend half their day waiting at checkpoints. Also, a series of invasions, most notably those in March and April 2002, were directed at destroying the administrative and physical apparatus of any conceivable Palestinian state.[15]

The "road map," promulgated in April 2003, is the logical next step. The culmination of a process started in 2002, it aims at re-creating a Palestinian client state, this time headed by Arafat's long-time associate Abu Mazen. His job will be to destroy Palestinian resistance[16] and to free the Israeli state to carry out its grander regional plans. His reward for this will be a seat at a new bargaining table, in which once again Palestinians will have no leverage. Even before the process started, Israeli Prime Minister Ariel Sharon was on record as saying, "If we reach a situation of true peace, real peace, peace for generations, we will have to make painful concessions. Not in exchange for promises, but rather in exchange for peace." In other words, no concrete concessions would be made until the Palestinians had completely capitulated and given up any chance of future resistance.[17] There is no doubt that a crucial component of these new plans is U.S. use of what nameless government officials quoted in the *Los Angeles Times* referred to as the "unspoken but obvious leverage of its new regional dominance."[18]

PLANS FOR THE UN

The United States is not just wielding a big stick in the Middle East, or against isolated nations like Syria. The war was also a springboard from which the United States could assert a much more overt dominance over the United Nations.

In its drive to war, the United States showed open contempt for the United Nations. On September 12, 2002, when Bush addressed the General Assembly, the message was, "The United Nations must do what we say or it risks becoming irrelevant." In late 2002 and early 2003, the U.N. became an unwitting accomplice in the war, disarming Iraq while the United States moved ahead with its military mobilization and war plans. Then, on March 16, 2003, Bush issued twin ultimata—one to Iraq to "disarm" in 24 hours, and the other to the U.N. to pass a resolution for war within 24 hours. When neither entity acceded to these demands, war was essentially declared on both.

Shortly after the United States went to war without U.N. approval, in blatant defiance of the unique authority granted to the Security Council, Richard Perle, then chair of the Defense Policy Board, published an op-ed in the *Guardian* entitled "Thank God for the death of the UN." In it, he said very openly that the "abject failure" of the U.N. gave the world anarchy and that the United States was the only fit guarantor of order. He defined the future role of the U.N. quite clearly: "The 'good works' part will survive, the low-risk peacekeeping bureaucracies will remain, the chatterbox on the Hudson will continue to bleat."[19]

In the following weeks, the Bush administration, while employing less violent rhetoric, moved to implement Perle's vision. George Bush, when pressed on the "vital role" he said the U.N. should be playing, said, "That means food. That means medicine. That means aid."[20] What that clearly did not mean was exercising any authority over the postwar ordering of Iraq.

Many of the supposed advocates of the U.N.'s authority did not really challenge this vision, except in detail. U.N. Secretary General Kofi Annan, for example, urged that the U.N. play a lead role in relief and reconstruction, adding that the involvement of the U.N. would "bring legitimacy" to the Iraqi government that was to be created.[21] Germany, a steadfast opponent of the war, suggested that it might play a role in reconstruction even if the U.N. was not in charge.[22] Others suggested that the U.N. even be given some nominal authority in the creation of the interim Iraqi government.

But none of them challenged the basic idea that Iraqi society would be reconstructed under U.S. military occupation. With the United States occupying the country, of course, any authority the U.N. might have on paper (most likely a joint authority with the occupying forces in any case) would be moot in practice, given the clear U.S. goals and the leverage its presence would give it.

In essence, what the United States was pushing for and what the supporters of the U.N. were implicitly agreeing to was casting the United Nations in the role of a subordinate agent of U.S. policy. Worse, the U.N. was to be an enabler for U.S. aggression—helping to clean up the mess, even for a war that it explicitly didn't authorize, thus freeing the United States to move on to project its force elsewhere.

The final straw came when the United States called for the sanctions to be lifted. For over a decade, every U.S. government official maintained that the regime, not the sanctions, was the cause of malnutrition and social decay in Iraq; miraculously, when the regime was gone, the United States suddenly discovered that sanctions were a problem, independent of regime. This development occasioned a complete role reversal, as France and Russia, the permanent members of the Security Council previously most opposed to the sanctions, initially called for their continuation. The reason for the switch was clear; the United States, in the process of creating the Iraqi government it wanted, wanted to make sure that the United Nations had no further power over Iraqi oil money, so that instead that power would be wielded, directly or indirectly, by the United States. In particular, the money would then be directly available to finance reconstruction projects, the lion's share of which were to go to American corporations.

Lifting of the sanctions should have been opposed on the basis that only a legitimate Iraqi government, and not one imposed by the U.S. military, should have unfettered access to the oil money. When Iraq invaded Kuwait, Kuwait's oil was included under the embargo, along with Iraqi oil, so that neither the Iraqi government nor the puppet government it tried to set up could plunder Kuwait's oil wealth for its own purposes; the principle with the U.S. invasion of Iraq is the same. Since other countries deemed it politically impossible to act on those grounds, they fell back on a legalistic attempt to require that U.N. weapons inspectors declare Iraq free of weapons of mass destruction. After initial opposition, as of this writing, France had already moved to suggest a compromise plan that would partly serve those U.S. goals.[23]

Using Iraq's oil money to finance basic humanitarian and reconstruction goals also clearly violates the obligation of the United States and United Kingdom under the Geneva Convention—having waged an aggressive war against Iraq, they were and are financially responsible for meeting those needs themselves.

The United States reached new heights of arrogance toward the U.N. when it refused to allow U.N. weapons inspections to resume after the war was over, instead taking over operations itself.[24]

EMPIRE CORRUPTS

The United States has reached a new zenith of political dominance—capable of flouting the express wishes of the vast mass of humanity and the vast majority of nations and still force them to assimilate into its ever-expanding structures of control. There is no longer any pretense that the United States is not an empire, or even that it is a reluctant one. For the apologists of the new order, the entire question hangs on not whether or not an empire exits, but whether or not the empire is benevolent.

For the rest of us, two things should be clear. First, that even the most benevolent empire is no substitute for independence and international equality. Second, that empires are never benevolent; the considerations of the empire-builders cannot possibly align with the considerations of the people being ruled.

As we will discover, the claims to benevolence of this empire ring particularly hollow.

THE "WAR ON TERRORISM"

CHAPTER 1

What It's Not—A War on Terrorism

IN MY BOOK, *The New Crusade: America's War on Terrorism*, (Monthly Review Press, 2002) completed in January 2002, I wrote: "The world changed on September 11. That's not just media hype. The way some historians refer to 1914–1991 as the 'short twentieth century,' many are now calling September 11, 2001 the real beginning of the twenty-first century. It's too early to know whether that assessment will be borne out, but it cannot simply be dismissed."

A few months later, it had already become crystal-clear that September 11, 2001 did, in fact, mark the beginning of a new era. The reason is not so much the attacks, horrific as they were (the death toll of some 3,000 represents the largest number killed instantly in a single criminal act perpetrated by non-state actors), nor even the repeated revelation of the threat posed by an international terrorist network; rather, the fundamental shift in world events comes from the response launched by the U.S. government—the so-called "war on terrorism."

In a sense, this book is about what the "war on terrorism" really is, with a heavy focus on Iraq, because Iraq has been and remains the centerpiece of the policy. First, though, one must discuss what it is not.

The "war on terrorism" is not a war on terrorism. From the very beginning, there were good reasons to believe that a militaristic response of the kind we have seen since 9/11 would not work and might well, in fact, exacerbate the threat. If the safety of ordinary Americans was a significant concern for the Bush administration, its policies would be very different.

On the domestic front, the negligence is stunning. Because of airline concerns about profitability, armored cockpit doors, which would have prevented the 9/11 attacks, have still not been installed on planes; even X-raying of checked bags at airports was not instituted on a wide scale until a full year after the attacks. Despite all the fanfare about "homeland security," minimal actions have been taken to provide local emergency services.

The domestic repression and targeting of Muslim communities, in addition to violating basic rights, has probably been counterproductive—the Justice Department dragnet that hauled in over 1,200 people, mostly for minor visa infractions, detaining many of them for months without charges, produced a total of one indictment on a terrorism-related charge. Some of those detained were people who had come forward to offer evidence to the FBI—their detention was an act almost calculated to exert a chilling effect on any attempts from the targeted communities (mostly those of Arab and South Asian descent) to aid affirmatively in the investigation.

It is, however, the Bush foreign policy that has been most detrimental to fighting the threat of al-Qaeda-style terrorism. The war on Afghanistan, judged purely as an anti-terrorist exercise, has been the worst failure of all. First, if you're trying to catch individuals, extradition has a much higher probability of success than war. Dropping 2,000-pound bombs is not the smartest way to go looking for criminals. It will kill a few of them, but not only will many innocent people get killed, the confusion and the hundreds of thousands of new refugees created by the bombing will allow small bands of well-organized people to slip away. And, in fact, the war did not result in the apprehension of Osama bin Laden or any other high-level al-Qaeda leader, although Mohammed Atef, one of the military leaders, was killed. In fact, the most significant members actually apprehended, like Abu Zubaydah and Khalid Shaikh Mohammed, were caught by undramatic, routine police operations.

Although many Americans swept up in a desire to avenge the dead of 9/11 may have been unable to use common sense, government planners must surely have known that the chance of apprehending the targeted men was greater through extradition than through war.

The standard line, and the common assumption, is that Taliban intransigence made extradition impossible. That's hardly the case. Shortly before the Afghanistan bombing started, the Taliban offered to turn bin Laden over to a neutral third country, even without hearing the evidence—even to allow him to be tried under Islamic law in the United States.[25] A week after the bombing started, when the offers were reiterated, Bush's response was: "There's no need to negotiate. There's no discussion. I told them exactly what they need to do. And there's no need to discuss innocence or guilt. We know he's guilty."

The peremptory demands, if anything, disposed the Taliban to go back on their initial offers. However, even after the Bush administration's repeated refusals to offer any evidence (the normal routine is to present evidence when requesting extradition), the Taliban was still ready to deal. In fact, shortly before the war was launched, a secret deal to turn over bin Laden had been agreed upon.[26] A delegation led by Qazi Hussain Ahmad, the Pakistani head of the fundamentalist Jamaat-i-Islami, had agreed with Mullah Omar, head of the then government of Afghanistan, that bin Laden would be taken to Pakistan, where, within the framework of Islamic law, evidence of his involvement would be placed before an international tribunal. The tribunal would decide whether to try him itself or hand him over to the United States. Even though the proposal had bin Laden's approval, it was turned down by President Pervez Musharraf of Pakistan on the bizarre grounds that he could not guarantee bin Laden's safety—an odd concern given the frequent calls from U.S. government officials to kill bin Laden instead of letting him be captured. Presumably, had the United States really wanted bin Laden extradited, it would not have allowed Musharraf to get in the way.

The central conclusion is clear: The United States took a course of action that gave bin Laden and others a higher chance of escaping, because extradition would have meant the absence of any *casus belli* (cause for war), and presumably the war was more important to the United States than their apprehension.

The handling of the bin Laden extradition is fairly typical of U.S. policy. It's certainly nothing peculiar to the Bush administration. In fact, throughout the 1990s, as conferences and military position papers and fear-mongering about the threat of terrorism proliferated, actual policies never seriously took safety into account.

On August 7, 1998, two U.S. embassies, in Kenya and Tanzania, were bombed, killing over 250 people (including 12 Americans). This was the incident that put al-Qaeda on the map worldwide, partly because of the U.S. response of plastering bin Laden's face on wanted posters all over the region. Two weeks after the attacks, Bill Clinton ordered the bombing of the El Shifa pharmaceutical plant in Sudan and of several "terrorist training camps" in Afghanistan (whose locations were known because they were largely CIA-created) in retaliation.

According to a report from MSNBC.com, "The day after the Aug. 7, 1998, attacks, two of the suspected bombers were arrested in Sudan, which then offered to turn them over to the FBI, according to accounts from two senior U.S. law enforcement officials and diplomatic sources."[27] The State Department prevented the FBI from following up on these leads. According to a senior FBI official, "The rationale was weak and it was, in my view, unconscionable. State simply would not let us even discuss the issue with the Sudanese."

No convincing reason for this refusal has been suggested. Of course, had the Clinton administration accepted these offers of cooperation from the Sudanese government, it would have been very difficult to bomb the El Shifa plant. The immediate rationales for bombing the plant were that it was owned indirectly by bin Laden and that it was manufacturing precursors for VX nerve gas, both of which claims were later shown to be false. Of course, the United States does not have the right to bomb any place involved in producing chemical weapons, but leaving that aside, if it had suspicions that this was going on, it could always have demanded inspections.

One person was killed directly in the bombing, but the total number who died because of it (and because of the U.S.'s continuing stubborn refusal to make any form of restitution) is presumably very high, in the thousands or tens of thousands, since El Shifa produced about 60 percent[28] of the pharmaceutical drugs used to combat the most deadly diseases facing the Sudanese, including malaria, tuberculosis, and cholera.

Once again, it's difficult to escape the conclusion that bombing the El Shifa plant was more important to the Clinton administration than reducing the threat of terrorist attacks against American civilians.

Even worse, from 1995 until weeks before the attacks of 9/11, the Clinton and Bush administrations repeatedly refused Sudanese offers to turn over their copious files on bin Laden. This refusal was termed "worse than a crime" by Tim Carney, the last U.S. ambassador to Sudan, who ended his posting in 1997. Given the nature of the Sudanese government's information, acceptance of this offer could have dramatically reduced the possibility of carrying out the attacks on U.S. embassies in 1998 and would at least have decreased the likelihood of success in the 9/11 attacks. According to the London based *Observer*, a CIA source lamented the refusal of the offer, stating, "This represents the worst single intelligence failure in this whole terrible business... It is reasonable to say that had we had this data we may have had a better chance of preventing the attacks."

Not only was the war in Afghanistan not the best way of capturing high-level al-Qaeda members, it actually dramatically exacerbated the threat from al-Qaeda and other Islamist formations. Early opponents of that war made the argument that the bombing would increase the threat of terrorism. At the time, very few agreed. In fact, many progressive intellectuals castigated the antiwar movement for what they considered its reflexive stupidity in opposing the war. A mere nine months after the beginning of the war, however, analysts at the FBI and CIA were among those who agreed with the antiwar movement—although many of the aforementioned intellectuals still did not. According to the *New York Times*, in June 2002, "Classified investigations of the Qaeda threat now underway at the FBI and CIA have concluded that the war in Afghanistan failed to diminish the threat to the United States... Instead, the war might have complicated counterterrorism efforts by dispersing potential attackers across a wider geographic area."[29]

Middle-level al-Qaeda operatives used the opportunity to strengthen contacts with other Islamist groups in the region. The war enabled them to draw these groups, hitherto focused on their own domestic political questions, into the world of terrorist networks opposing the United States—thus dramatically increasing the pool from which future terrorists will be drawn. According to one official, "Al-Qaeda at its core was really a small group, even though thousands of people went through their camps. What we're seeing now is a radical international jihad that will be a potent force for many years to come."

The bombing of a nightclub in Bali on October 12, 2002, which killed 192 people (nearly all Westerners, with Australians the largest single group of victims), brought the absurdity of this approach to the "war on terrorism" into the sharpest relief.

Military policy analysts have understood for years that it is the very predominance of the U.S. military that makes opponents or potential opponents of U.S. policies turn to "asymmetric warfare," in which that tremendous technological and material advantage can be partially neutralized, as it was on 9/11. The government had acknowledged this fact by the '90s, for example, in Presidential Decision Directive 62: "America's unrivaled military superiority means that potential enemies (whether nations or terrorist groups) that choose to attack us will be more likely to resort to terror instead of conventional military assault."[30]

Clearly, the steps since 9/11 to increase that military superiority even more and to use it more frequently represent exactly the wrong approach, and will dramatically exacerbate the threat of terrorism.

The Bali attack is clearly one of the fruits of the Afghanistan war—a suspect in custody has admitted that it was aimed at Americans, not Australians.[31]

It also represents a significant change in terrorist tactics. Contrary to the popular conception of al-Qaeda as simply ravening to kill Americans any chance it gets, the organization never previously went for easy "soft" targets. The list of attacks by al-Qaeda—two U.S. embassies, the *USS Cole*, the World Trade Center and Pentagon—shows a pattern of hard targets that symbolize U.S. power, involving difficult preparation and people willing to commit suicide. The Bali nightclub was a soft target of no particular symbolic value. Suspects reportedly said that senior al-Qaeda members, meeting in Thailand in January 2002, "decided to turn from embassies, which were becoming better protected, to so called soft targets like resorts and schools."[32] Thus, the war on terrorism reaches its *reductio ad absurdum*—more military prowess leads to more terrorist attacks, more defense of hard targets leads to more attacks on soft targets, and it is simply impossible to defend all soft targets.

Given the deliberate refusal to consider potential information about bin Laden and al-Qaeda, and the adoption of a course of action (war) that actually increases the threat of terrorist attacks, it's difficult to escape the conclusion that fighting terrorism, even specifically radical Islamist terrorism, is not a priority for the U.S. government, even after 9/11.

One could conclude that the "war on terrorism" is no more about fighting terrorism than the "war on drugs" is about fighting drug use. Any serious study has concluded that, dollar for dollar, by far the best return in lowering drug use is obtained by making treatment available, yet the United States still doesn't even provide treatment on demand for all who request it. The main motivations for the drug war are domestic militarization and control of what is being constituted as a permanent racial underclass, while simultaneously extending U.S. military influence in all of South America, with Colombia as a primary staging area. In each case, it is not as if the government actually wants greater drug use or more terrorist attacks; rather, it has little direct concern about those questions, wishing to address them only as rhetorical justification for militaristic "solutions."

CHAPTER 2

A New Imperialism?

Understanding the Bush National Security Strategy

SO IF THE WAR on terrorism is not a war on terrorism, what is it? It can be fruitfully understood as a new Cold War, with terrorism replacing communism as the omnipresent threat against which we must defend.

Starting shortly after the 9/11 attacks, Bush administration officials moved to drive home to the public the point that a new era had been entered, and that the country was at war for the foreseeable future. Vice President Dick Cheney, announcing the lifting of the 25-year executive ban on assassinations in the case of Osama bin Laden, said that the war on terrorism was "different than the Gulf War was, in the sense that it may never end. At least, not in our lifetime."[33]

In accordance with the unwritten rule that every president gets a doctrine if he wants one, Bush promulgated the Bush Doctrine: "Either you are with us, or you are with the terrorists. From this day forward, any nation that continues to harbor or support terrorism will be regarded by the United States as a hostile regime."[34] This is an obvious successor to the famed Truman Doctrine, which essentially says the United States has a right to intervene, and a compelling interest in intervening, in any country where Communists are gaining political power (in practice, in any country where the United States could claim there was some threat of Communist political influence—something it routinely did in countries which showed even a slight potential for the development of independent policy).

The 2002 State of the Union address outlined the ideological superstructure of this new Cold War, embodying the same stark vision of war between light and darkness, civilization and barbarism that permeates Paul Nitze's NSC-68, often considered the foundational document of the Cold War. The United States, along with the rest of the "civilized world," is on a higher moral plane, opposed to the "axis of evil," which includes Iran, Iraq, North Korea, and unnamed "terrorist allies." The crusade to which we are called is couched in universalist terms— "the rule of law, limits on the power of the state, respect for women, private property, free speech, equal justice and religious tolerance"—but the cultural supremacism is only thinly veiled.

The speech fleshes out further this analogy with the omni-interventionism of the Truman Doctrine: "Some governments will be timid in the face of terror. And make no mistake: If they do not act, America will." The war on terrorism, like the war on communism, is a doctrinal system in which any development anywhere can be deemed a potential threat to our national security. From this follows another Cold War standard, expressed in the speech—the need for permanently higher military budgets in order to "defend" ourselves.

It also invokes the omnipresent internal enemy—"and as government works to better secure our homeland, America will continue to depend on the eyes and ears of alert citizens." How to tell if your neighbor is a terrorist replaces how to tell if your neighbor is a communist.

It's often been noted that a "search for enemies" is a necessary part of U.S. foreign policy; there's a need to justify incredible levels of military spending even as the United States has a near-monopoly on military power, and maintenance of U.S. world dominance occasionally requires that some seemingly recalcitrant state be battered into submission. Although there are examples where any enemy would do, in many cases, as we'll see later, we already know who the enemies are—countries with important strategic resources and some potential for independent policy.

Many "enemies" have been tried out since the fall of the Soviet Union—rogue states, narcotraffickers—but al-Qaeda-style global terrorism fits the bill much better. Fighting terrorism, like fighting communism before it, becomes the perfect justification for intervening in the countries the United States wanted to intervene in anyway.

THE NATIONAL SECURITY STRATEGY AND THE
PROJECT FOR THE NEW AMERICAN CENTURY

We can see the structure of the emerging foreign policy in much more detail by examining two closely linked documents, the Bush administration's recently (September 2002) promulgated National Security Strategy (NSS)[35] and "Rebuilding America's Defenses: Strategy, Forces and Resources for a New Century" (RAD), put out by the Project for the New American Century (PNAC) in September 2000.[36]

Both documents can trace their roots back to the "Defense Planning Guidance" written in 1992 by Deputy Defense Secretary Paul Wolfowitz, then Number 3 in the Defense Department, and I. Lewis Libby, now Vice President Cheney's chief of staff. So stark was its vision of unilateral military domination by the United States, without even lip service to the fiction that the United States is merely *primus inter pares* (first among equals) with respect to its allies, that the government was forced to repudiate it and have it rewritten with a more multilateral flavor before release. Now, the original rhetoric can be more openly embraced.

The name "Project for the New American Century" harkens back to Henry Luce's prophetic 1941 proclamation of the twentieth century as the "American century." The group is a private think-tank concerned, as the name suggests, with maintaining and extending U.S. world dominance. It's not just any think-tank, however; its board includes neoconservative leading lights like William Kristol and Robert Kagan, as well as John Bolton, now undersecretary of state for arms control. It was prepared with the input, *inter alia*, of Wolfowitz, Libby, Dov Zakheim (now chief financial officer for the Defense Department), and Eliot Cohen and Devon Cros, who serve on the advisory Defense Policy Board then chaired by Richard Perle.

"Rebuilding America's Defenses" came to the public's attention with the publication on September 15, 2002, of an article in the *Scotland Sunday Herald*[37] luridly proclaiming that the document was Bush's "secret blueprint for U.S. global domination." Although it's not quite that, it does shed a great deal of light on post–9/11 policy decisions and helps to flesh out the rather scanty NSS, which reads like a collection of press releases.

The NSS starts off with a straightforward proclamation of the new challenges to "national security": "Enemies in the past needed great armies and great industrial capabilities to endanger America. Now, shadowy networks of individuals can bring great chaos and suffering to our shores for less than it costs to purchase a single tank." It states clearly the problem of asymmetric warfare: "Terrorists are organized... to turn the power of modern technologies against us."[38] After this, one is hard-pressed to find anything dealing with the threat of al-Qaeda–style terrorism anywhere in the document.

Instead, we find a recipe for the United States somehow to solve all its problems by exacerbating all the reasons for them—by a further extension of its military dominance and a more aggressive approach toward countries that get in the way of "U.S. interests." It calls for openly basing U.S. global hegemony on complete American military dominance, relative not only to enemies but to allies as well: "our military must… dissuade future military competition."[39]

It is here that it dovetails strongly with "Rebuilding America's Defenses" (RAD), which is essentially a blueprint for a new post–Cold-War American military and foreign policy that is structured to take advantage of the "unipolar moment." It is intended to sound the alarm against all of those (including, according to the document, Bill Clinton and his advisers) who saw the end of the Cold War as the opportunity for a "strategic pause" in which the United States could rest on its laurels (and its overwhelming military superiority). Instead, the end of any potentially meaningful military opposition to U.S. power calls, in the minds of the neoconservatives, for increased military spending and a dramatic transformation of both military technology and the role of the military: "Preserving the desirable strategic situation in which the United States now finds itself requires a globally preeminent military capability both today and in the future."[40]

During the Cold War, especially in the '60s and the '80s, it was a commonplace technique to justify new weapons programs by claiming that the Soviet Union was ahead of the United States, that there was for example, a "missile gap." Those claims were absurd, and U.S. military planners knew they were, but they preserved the posture of U.S. military policy as being primarily defensive against the Soviet threat. With the new National Security Strategy, the gloves are off—although we admit that nobody comes close to us militarily, we intend to accelerate our buildup so that no one can ever imagine rivaling us militarily and challenging our hegemony.

The authors of RAD note that this whole revolutionary transformation of the military and its role seems to be politically impossible in the climate of 2000, "absent some catastrophic and catalyzing event—like a new Pearl Harbor."[41] At that time, the authors must have despaired of the possibility, but within a year they had their Pearl Harbor and the chance to turn their imperial fantasies into reality. Conspiracy theorists will no doubt rejoice, but this, like so many events in the history of U.S. foreign policy, is simply another example of Pasteur's famous axiom that "Fortune favors the prepared mind."

In this stark military vision of world domination, China inevitably looms large as a country not in the U.S. sphere and with a fully developed military deterrent. In fact, according to RAD it will be America's primary strategic challenge in the near future. Consonant with Zbigniew Brzezinski's analysis in his book *The Grand*

Chessboard that reunification of Korea would be a problem for U.S. strategic interests because the United States needs an excuse to keep troops in the area to bottle up China and keep Japan in its sphere of influence, RAD suggests that, although "conventional wisdom has it that the 37,000-man U.S. garrison in South Korea is merely there to protect against the possibility of an invasion from the North," and "Korean unification might call for the reduction in American presence on the peninsula and a transformation of U.S. force posture in Korea," what would be needed is "a *change* in their mission... not the *termination* of their mission."[42]

THE NEW IMPERIALISM

From these two documents, one can discern the central principles of the neoconservative vision:

> ➤ Military transformation, i.e., massive spending to upgrade military technology so as to further increase America's already unquestioned superiority.
> ➤ Military bases, i.e., the continued expansion throughout the world of an American military presence that was already at its greatest global reach and dispersion everywhere—"the United States should seek to establish a network of 'deployment bases' or 'forward operating bases'

to increase the reach of current and future forces." They are to be a primary element of U.S. political hegemony over both the countries hosting the bases and over the countries menaced by them.

➤ "Regime change," i.e., the overt establishment of governments that are strongly beholden to the U.S. military and thus under the more or less direct control of the United States. In this regard, there is a need for a military transformation strategy to take account of the greater requirements imposed by frequent regime change and postwar military occupation—"past Pentagon wargames have given little or no consideration to the force requirements necessary not only to defeat an attack but to remove these regimes [Iraq and North Korea] from power and conduct post-combat stability operations."[43]

Left conspicuously out of these documents is the fourth component, broadly hinted at in the Bush-Cheney energy policy: maximal control over the production and transportation of oil.

Put them all together, and we see the broad contours of imperial strategy emerging out of the wreckage of the World Trade Center.

THE NEOCONSERVATIVE OBSESSION WITH MISSILE DEFENSE

One of the most interesting and crucial insights afforded by RAD is an explanation of the recent obsession with "national missile defense."

According to the World Policy Institute, since Reagan's inauguration of the original "Star Wars" program in 1983, $70 billion has been spent on missile defense. Over that time, the project has been scaled down from a defense against a Soviet first strike involving 10,000 warheads to one involving about 20 missiles. The Congressional Budget Office estimates that current plans will require another $60 billion—some independent estimates double that figure.

After 9/11, one of the first reactions was an increase in the appropriation for missile defense, even though no one was under any illusion that it would have made a difference in an attack of the kind seen then or envisioned thereafter.

In all recent incarnations, it has been sold as a defense against "rogue states" like Iran, Iraq, and North Korea, who form the current "axis of evil." None of these states has the capacity to attack the United States with even a single missile, and only North Korea could conceivably gain such a capacity in the next 15 years. Even if any of these states did gain such a limited capacity, the certainty of massive swift retribution would make any strike prohibitively unlikely.

Searching to make sense of the policy, several commentators have pointed to the fact that 20 intercontinental missiles is just about the size of China's long-range nuclear arsenal. Combining this with the fact that 100 percent success in interception is impossible, they have been led to the idea that missile defense has another goal—to shield a first-strike capability. If the United States launched a massive first strike, destroying 19 of 20 ICBM's, it could hope that the missile defense system might take out the one remaining missile in flight.

China has certainly seen the program that way; before 9/11, it exacerbated tension with the United States, already severe since the 1999 U.S. strike on the Chinese embassy in Belgrade. George W. Bush even admitted in August 2001 that China might feel this threat and that the United States will understand if China wishes to build more and better intercontinental missiles, which, of course, undercuts the whole logic of any missile defense aimed against China. Worse, a Chinese buildup could set off a drive by India to build a similar arsenal, which would then require Pakistan to respond. Overall, the policy has seemed strategically counterproductive, in addition to extremely expensive.

Because of these puzzling features, peace activists have often assumed it is simply a huge corporate boondoggle of some sort, an impression strengthened by scientific assessments that current missile defense plans, based on use of an exo-atmospheric "kill vehicle" to intercept a high-speed intercontinental ballistic missile in full flight, are technically unfeasible at this time, and by revelations that the "successful" tests were actually rigged.[44]

Peace Action, a group to which I belong, had a "Star Wars is a Lemon" campaign based on this idea—that it was a waste of money on something that wouldn't work. More recently, Peace Action has unveiled a series of ads in the Washington *Metro* calling missile defense "Enron in Space," complete with pictures of bloated pigs sailing peacefully into the void.

The truth is somewhat different. RAD explains the policy by returning the focus to the "rogue states," but not in the way that is usually reported. In a remarkable admission, it states:

> In the post–Cold-War era, America and its allies, rather than the Soviet Union, have become the primary objects of deterrence and it is states like Iraq, Iran and North Korea who most wish to develop deterrent capabilities. Projecting conventional military forces or simply asserting political influence abroad, particularly in times of crisis, will be far more complex and constrained when the American homeland or the territory of our allies is subject to attack by otherwise weak rogue regimes capable of cobbling together a miniscule ballistic missile force. Building an effective, robust, layered, global sys-

tem of missile defenses is a prerequisite for maintaining American preeminence.[45]

Of course, during the Cold War, it was also true that America was "the primary object of deterrence," but it was never stated so openly in a publicly available document.

Missile defense is needed to enable us to attack other countries with impunity—in particular, it is necessary so that small weak countries cannot deter American aggression with the threat of any consequences either to American allies in the region or to forward-based American troops.

What is needed is a global system with "theater-wide" components based around the world, "Thus the requirement for upper-tier, theater-wide defenses like the Army's Theater High Altitude Area Defense (THAAD) and the Navy Theater-Wide systems."[46] Theater defense systems with interceptors of the high speeds envisioned require the scrapping of limits set in the ABM treaty, explaining why the Bush administration pushed forward with such a clearly destabilizing move.

Again, the document is quite open: "In fact, it is misleading to think of such a system as a 'national' missile defense system, for it would be a vital element in theater defenses, protecting U.S. allies or expeditionary forces abroad from longer-range theater weapons."[47] In other words, missile defense has nothing whatsoever to do with national defense.

A *NEW* NEW WORLD ORDER

All in all, a frightening picture. American political dominance must be based on overwhelming military superiority, reinforced periodically by small "theater wars" fought against foes that are helpless to resist, to be followed potentially by American military occupation and installation of regimes that will obey American dictates. It goes without saying that American ideas of economic system and policy will be imposed in this process, just as in Bosnia, whose U.S.-imposed constitution commits it to the "free market" and requires that the head of the Central Bank be non-Bosnian. Indeed, according to the NSS, "lower marginal tax rates" and "pro-growth legal and regulatory policies to encourage business investment" in foreign countries are essential to our national security.

In RAD, this picture is unleavened by any invocation, no matter how spurious, of a serious threat posed by any of these states—on the contrary, it is understood that "America and its allies... have become the primary objects of deterrence." Presumably because it was prepared when the neoconservatives were out of power, it is far more honest than most openly obtainable documents that are so clearly linked to current government policy. Its frequent invocations of "the American peace" can only be read as a recipe for a Pax Americana in the imperial sense and not as having anything to do with peace: "If an American peace is to be maintained, and expanded, it must have a secure foundation on unquestioned U.S. military preeminence."[48]

This stark picture of plans for unprovoked aggression in pursuit of American world dominance is leavened only slightly by the NSS, which contains a tortured attempt to justify these plans by invoking the already infamous preemption doctrine. Recognizing correctly that "traditional concepts of deterrence will not work against a terrorist enemy... whose most potent protection is statelessness,"[49] it goes on to logically leap tall buildings with a single bound, claiming that this consideration requires the unprovoked targeting of small, weak, eminently deterrable states, none of which could conceivably withstand an American military attack.

Instead of following this insight to the obvious conclusion that traditional ideas of war don't work very well against stateless multinational terrorist networks, it opportunistically seizes on the 9/11 attacks to tie completely unrelated, and even diametrically opposed, plans for a hyperaggressive foreign policy to the need to protect people from terrorist attacks.

Given these plans for repeated open aggression by the United States, it is no surprise that subversion of the International Criminal Court (ICC) and renunciation of any concept of international accountability for the United States is an essential part of this new policy. Not only has the United States not ratified the treaty creating the court, the National Security Strategy takes us a step further:

"We will take the actions necessary to ensure that our efforts to meet our global security commitments and protect Americans are not impaired by the potential for investigations, inquiry, or prosecution by the International Criminal Court (ICC), whose jurisdiction does not extend to Americans and which we do not accept."[50]

The United States has already concluded bilateral agreements with Afghanistan, the Dominican Republic, East Timor, The Gambia, Honduras, Israel, the Marshall Islands, Mauritania, Micronesia, Palau, Romania, Tajikistan, Uzbekistan, Kuwait, and India,[51] in which each side agrees not to extradite the other's nationals for trial before the International Criminal Court.

The American Servicemembers Protection Act is known to many insiders as the "Invade the Hague" Act because it authorizes the president to go to war to prevent American personnel from being tried in international courts. Despite the numerous protestations of concern for ordinary American soldiers, the real concern with regard to the ICC is the potential trial of Henry Kissinger—and perhaps of Bush, Cheney, Rumsfeld, and others in the near future. Indeed, according to the *New York Times*, "In most of their public utterances, administration officials have argued that they feared American soldiers might be subject to politically motivated charges. But in private discussions with allies, officials say, they are now stressing deep concerns about the vulnerability of top civilian leaders to international legal action."[52]

A recipe for aggression is not complete without a strategy for impunity.

CHAPTER 3

A Survey of U.S. Foreign Policy Since 9/11

THE ATTACKS OF 9/11 provided the neoconservatives with their new Pearl Harbor—the perfect opportunity for the Bush administration to start realizing the vision laid out above, relatively unfettered by the considerations that prevailed in the pre-9/11 world. Within hours of the attacks, they set about their task of reshaping the world.

WEAPONS, MISSILE DEFENSE, AND NUCLEAR DOMINANCE

The 9/11 attacks were a natural opportunity to jack up the military budget. The White House military budget request for fiscal 2004 totaled $399.1 billion.[53] This represents roughly a 30 percent increase from the late '90s, taking spending considerably above the level envisioned by the PNAC, which had not foreseen 9/11 and therefore could not have expected that higher budgets would be feasible.

There has also been a shift from the long-term policy

of nuclear deterrence to a new one of nuclear dominance. The *Nuclear Posture Review*, a classified Pentagon study that was communicated to Congress on December 31, 2001, from which time a number of its findings leaked into the public sphere, made headlines with its statement that the United States should be prepared to target up to seven countries—China, Russia, Iraq, North Korea, Iran, Libya and Syria—with nuclear weapons. John Bolton, undersecretary of state for arms control, explicitly affirmed this implicit admission that the United States was dropping its pledge not to use nuclear weapons on non-nuclear states, explaining, "We are just not into theoretical assertions that other administrations have made."

The *Nuclear Posture Review* also calls for the development of a new generation of nuclear weapons, the so-called "bunker busters." These low-yield earth-penetrating weapons are ostensibly designed to destroy deeply buried and/or hardened structures, particularly potential caches of weapons of mass destruction or plants for their production, without harming any surface-dwelling civilian population. Aside from the fact that any use of nuclear weapons is (almost) universally condemned by the international community and a violation of international law, scientists dispute the idea that it is possible to contain the effects so neatly. According to Stephen Schwartz, writing in the *Bulletin of the Atomic Scientists*, even the effects of exploding a tiny 0.1–kiloton weapon, less than 1/100th the yield of the bomb dropped on Hiroshima, could not possibly be contained underground:

> Consider the planners' idea that smaller nuclear weapons could be used to hit underground targets without causing above-ground damage. To be fully contained, a 100-ton burrowing "mini-nuke" targeted against a hardened underground bunker would have to penetrate 230 feet underground (through soil, solid rock, and reinforced concrete) before exploding, a feat that is physically impossible.[54]

Other plans in the *Nuclear Posture Review* include $15 million for resumed use of the Nevada Test Site and an upgrading of the standard "nuclear triad"—submarine-based missiles, land-based missiles, and nuclear-capable strategic bombers.[55]

Putting these elements together is not difficult. As discussed earlier, because of the high failure rate, missile defense may make technical sense to shield a first strike of one's own, but not really to defend against a full first strike by an enemy. The development of the bunker-buster is an attempt to make a first strike more politically feasible, because one can claim (whether it's true or not) that such a weapon is harmless, not a "real" nuclear weapon. The renunciation of the pledge not to strike non-nuclear nations is a necessary step in using such a weapon. The release of an explicit target list that includes China, the main strategic concern of the neo-conservatives, as well as most of the list of "rogue states" the United States seems to be gunning for anyway, completes the picture of a transition to an overt policy of nuclear dominance based on a politically and militarily credible threat of a nuclear first strike. Whether such a threat would ever be actualized may not be the most important aspect—clearly, the plan is to use this credible threat for political leverage and control.

BASES AND OIL

The Bush administration telescoped about ten years of expansion and meddling into the year after 9/11, virtually all of it done explicitly in the name of the war on terrorism, but in fact revolving around the previously identified themes of bases, regime change, and oil.

As early as January 2002, military analyst William Arkin noted the theme of bases:

> Since Sept. 11, according to Pentagon sources, military tent cities have sprung up at 13 locations in nine countries neighboring Afghanistan, substantially extending the network of bases in the region. All together, from Bulgaria and Uzbekistan to Turkey, Kuwait and beyond, more

than 60,000 U.S. military personnel now live and work at these forward bases. Hundreds of aircraft fly in and out of so-called "expeditionary airfields."[56]

He went on to add, "While these bases make it easier for the United States to project its power, they may also increase prospects for renewed terrorist attacks on Americans."

Since then, the new network of bases and U.S. troop deployments has expanded considerably in numerous areas of the world. Military control of the flow of oil is manifesting in two ways—potential control over oil-producing countries, so the flow can be controlled at the source, and control over the worldwide transportation of oil through naval domination of key "chokepoints" through which much of the world's tanker traffic must flow.

CENTRAL ASIA

Let's start with Central Asia. Much has already been written of the importance of a U.S. presence in Afghanistan because of plans to build a natural gas pipeline from Turkmenistan, which has the world's third-largest reserves, through Afghanistan. Those plans were shelved in 1998, with the Clinton administration's cruise missile strikes on Afghanistan and the recognition that the political stability necessary to such commercial enterprises was likely to remain lacking.

There is also the question of oil pipelines from the rich, largely untapped reserves of the Caspian basin (the countries bordering the Caspian are Russia, Azerbaijan, Iran, Turkmenistan, and Kazakhstan) to markets with rapidly growing demand in East and South Asia. Iran is undoubtedly the best route for any such pipeline, since there is already an infrastructure to get oil pumped in Iran to tankers in the Persian Gulf and then to the world, but the United States has put itself squarely against Iran, first with the trade and investment sanctions levied in 1996, and more recently with the inclusion of Iran in the "axis of evil." An overland pipeline to China would be very long and would add significantly to the cost of the oil. A pipeline through Afghanistan is not a great solution, since the country is far from achieving any political stability, but some have seen it as the best solution in an imperfect world.

There has also been much vituperative criticism of that analysis of Afghanistan's strategic significance, for example from Ken Silverstein in the *American Prospect*. Much of the debate has missed the main points, however. True, the war on Afghanistan gave the United States control of the Afghan government (as we will see later, the sham of "democracy" the United States has put in there is feeble even by the standards of U.S.-created show democracies), but far more important is the fact that it has created a permanent U.S. military presence throughout the region.

In Afghanistan that presence includes 5,000 troops at the old Russian airbase at Bagram and another 3-4,000 in Kandahar, as well as numerous smaller deployments. In Pakistan, the United States has taken an airfield in Jacobabad for its own use, in addition to partial use of other fields—this is "part of what one Pakistani source predicts will become a 'semipermanent presence' of U.S. forces in Pakistan."[57] This presence also includes a series of permanent and semipermanent bases as well as various bilateral agreements which allow for the use of landing strips, bases and facilities in surrounding countries, especially Tajikistan, Kyrgyzstan, Uzbekistan, and Turkmenistan. (An excellent detailed description may be found in "Operation Endless Deployment," an article published in *The Nation*.[58])

U.S. presence in the region drives a military wedge between China and Russia. It also gives the U.S. military leverage over the oil of Central Asia, which might one day become an important source for China and Japan.

SOUTHEAST ASIA

Moving south, we find an unprecedented level of U.S.-Indian military cooperation, with large joint exercises involving army, air force, and navy, and a resumption of U.S. military sales to India. Most significant, the U.S. and

Indian navies are jointly patrolling the Straits of Malacca,[59] one of the three primary chokepoints for world oil flow—25 percent of what is shipped goes through the strait. Virtually all oil going to Japan passes through the straits. With China's demand for oil projected to grow far faster than its production capacity, China will also become heavily dependent on the straits. The United States thus has potential control over the flow of oil to those countries and therefore political power over them.

One of the early responses of the Bush administration to 9/11 was to seek to undo congressional restrictions on U.S. military connections with Indonesia, imposed largely because of the success grassroots activists had in highlighting Indonesia's horrible abuses in its occupation of East Timor (which ended in 1999). In the aftermath of the Bali bombing, with Indonesia fully signed on to the "war on terrorism," resumption of high-level cooperation is once again on the agenda.

The U.S. military has also gone back to the Philippines. They were formally released from colonial status in 1946, but remained in a very explicit neocolonial relationship to the United States long after. Most Filipinos date Philippine independence not to 1946 but to 1991, when a massive popular movement essentially forced the Philippine government to kick the U.S. military out of its major bases, including Clark and Subic Bay. At that time, the Philippine constitution was amended to prohibit the presence of foreign troops, except in transit and for training exercises.

From February through July 2002, over 1,300 U.S. soldiers were in the Philippines, ostensibly helping the Philippine military to hunt down the Abu Sayyaf group, a small collection of bandits and kidnappers allegedly part of the global terrorist threat facing Americans. In fact, there is much reason to suspect that the true target of joint U.S.-Filipino operations is quite different. After a visit by Secretary of State Colin Powell in August, the government of Gloria Macapagal-Arroyo declared "all-out war" on the Communist Party of the Philippines (CPP) and its armed wing, the New People's Army (NPA)—and virtually at the same time Powell added those two groups to the State Department's list of "foreign terrorist organizations." Popular resistance to a U.S. military role forced a delay in plans to deploy U.S. troops in the spring of 2003—in the end, 1,200 soldiers arrived in April 2003, but the government of Gloria Macapagal-Arroyo was forced to deny them any direct role in combat.[60]

THE MIDDLE EAST AND THE BALKANS

The United States has had a major land-based military presence in the Middle East, especially in the Persian Gulf region, ever since the Gulf War. Since 9/11, that presence has grown. As of March 2003, in numerous bases in the Gulf region, the U.S. deployment exceeded 250,000 troops. Permanent bases include three in Oman, a much upgraded and expanded al-Udeid in Qatar, bases in Kuwait, Bahrain, and Saudi Arabia, and a new Special Forces deployment in Djibouti. With this, the United States has a military presence abutting Bab el Mandeb Strait (connecting the Red Sea to the Gulf of Aden) as well as at the Straits of Hormuz (connecting the Persian Gulf to the Sea of Oman), two of the major chokepoints for world oil traffic.

Since 9/11, the United States has also moved to deploy Special Forces in Georgia, and to train an anti-terrorist force to patrol the Pankisi Gorge, an alleged refuge for al-Qaeda elements and for Chechen fighters. It's also worth mentioning the giant Camp Bondsteel in Kosovo, which has 7,000 troops stationed, and whose existence is one of the primary consequences of the Yugoslavia war. Its proximity to the planned Trans-Balkan AMBO (Albania, Macedonia, Bulgaria Oil) pipeline, which will bring Caspian oil from Black Sea ports to the Adriatic Sea without having to pass through the highly congested Bosporus trait, is notable.[61] Redeployment of European-based U.S. forces to southeastern Europe is one of the key necessities noted in "Rebuilding America's Defenses," and is an essential part of bringing Eastern Europe directly under the U.S. "security umbrella."

COLOMBIA

U.S. intervention in Colombia brings together the themes of suppressing armed popular resistance movements and oil. For several years, the United States has given major support to organized state terror in Colombia under the guise of a "drug war." This has involved massive defoliation campaigns reminiscent of Vietnam, in which not only coca crops but many normal food crops are destroyed; experimental use of a biological defoliant, "Agent Green" has been proposed.[62] During this time, tens of thousands of Colombians have been killed, over two million made into internal refugees, and the social fabric of much of rural Colombia destroyed.

Since 9/11, the counterdrug efforts have been completely recast. In November, U.S. Special Forces began "training" the Colombian military in counterinsurgency, in accord with an explicit 2002 budget appropriation of $94 million to help protect the Cano-Limon pipeline, which carries 100,000 barrels a day to the coast of Colombia for Occidental Petroleum.[63] Seen as a symbol of foreign domination, the pipeline has been bombed over 900 times since the early 1980s by the FARC and the ELN, which also extract oil royalty payments from local government officials.

VENEZUELA: "REGIME CHANGE" AND THE ASSAULT ON DEMOCRACY

U.S. operations in Venezuela, a major oil-producing country, after 9/11 have been perhaps the most revealing of all. Anyone who followed *New York Times* coverage of the presidency of Hugo Chávez Frias knew that Chávez was likely to be a primary target for U.S. attempts at "regime change," an understanding made explicit by pronouncements shortly after installation of the Bush administration.

People who attempted to understand Venezuela and the Chávez phenomenon simply by reading mainstream media reports could have been forgiven if they thought that he was a military dictator hated by the population, a consistent impression projected especially in the coverage by the *New York Times*. When there was a coup attempt on April 12, in fact, both the *Times* and the State Department initially reacted by hailing the coup as a victory for democracy—even though the first action of the coup leader, the "responsible businessman" Pedro Carmona Estanga, was to dissolve the National Assembly.

After the news got out that Chávez had been elected (with 62 percent of the vote) and after a spontaneous popular uprising helped put this "hated man" back in power, the powers-that-be in the United States were forced to recant and admit that a coup is not a good way to remove a democratically-elected government. One Bush administration official, however, hastened to add that Chávez should understand that "legitimacy is something that is conferred not just by a majority of the voters"[64]—an area where the Bush administration should have an especially keen insight.

Since then, it has (very quickly) transpired that the

United States did not just welcome the coup attempt with open arms. It actively fostered the coup. The National Endowment for Democracy (NED), which, as the name suggests, is a quasi-governmental organization designed to subvert democracy in other countries, gave $877,000 to anti-Chavez forces over the course of the year leading up to the coup.[65] Among the NED's other exploits is the buying of the 2000 elections in Yugoslavia, where it spent roughly $25 million dollars to support opposition groups against Milosevic.[66]

According to Stratfor, the private military intelligence corporation (http://www.stratfor.com), the CIA had been working on organizing oil union leaders and military commanders against Chávez since the summer of 2001. Otto Reich, assistant secretary of state for Western Hemisphere affairs and one of the Reagan administration's point men in its Central American operations, met several times with coup leaders and advised Carmona during the coup attempt—he claims, of course, that he knew nothing of the attempt.[67]

Chávez had long been a target, not so much for his actions against the Venezuelan oligarchy, but for his actions affecting the world oil market. Venezuela under Chávez has returned to its original role of fostering cooperation between oil-producing nations (Venezuela is the actual founder of OPEC), and played an instrumental role in bringing the price of oil back from its low of $7 per barrel in 1998. Chávez has also moved toward solidarity with non–oil-producing nations, giving Cuba oil at cut-rate prices, and has moved to increase the royalties foreign companies like Exxon-Mobil have to pay for Venezuelan oil.

Venezuela shows most clearly that "regime change" has nothing to do with installing democracy (in a slightly less direct way, so do Afghanistan, Iraq, and Palestine). The key question for U.S. planners is still, as it has been for a long time, how to minimize the potential for independent policy in the rest of the world, especially in the Third World.

THE WAR ON IRAQ

If the Bush foreign policy is characterized by an emphasis on "regime change," expansion of military bases, and control over the production and transport of oil, it was epitomized by the war on Iraq, which combined all three considerations right in the heart of the region that contains two-thirds of the world's oil reserves.

Of course, these "strategic" interests were never invoked by the Bush administration. Countries that regularly make war far from their borders tend to rely rhetorically, if not actually, on some kind of moral framework of justification; the United States is no exception.

Many of the arguments for the war have been obviated by events; in particular, the claim that Iraq posed some threat to the United States has been exposed as untenable. Still, a proper evaluation of the real reasons for the war requires a retrospective analysis of the justifications given. They must be judged not only with regard to what has been discovered since but with regard to what was or might have been known before the war started—obviously, decisions can be justified only on the basis of what is known, not what may be learned later.

There were two main categories of argument for the war. The first, focused on almost exclusively by the Bush administration until the last few weeks, derived from the threat that Iraq supposedly posed to the United States, to Americans, or possibly to unspecified "U.S. interests." The source of the threat was Iraq's supposed arsenal of weapons of mass destruction (WMD), combined with Saddam's propensity to use them, even, in the incessant refrain, "on his own people." These putative weapons were to play a role either through Iraq's giving them to al-Qaeda or similar terrorist organizations for use on American targets, or, in some nebulous and unspecified manner, through Iraq's direct use of them against Americans. Although the latter would only be a possibility at some way off time in the future, for the duration of the inspection process (re-started in November 2002) the United States constantly attempted to create a feeling of immediate urgency. Both possibilities were intimately tied in with the Bush "pre-emption doctrine," the idea that there is a right to attack countries which may conceivably develop the capacity and intent to pose a threat at some time in the future. Invocation of "pre-emption" was necessary because for a decade Iraq manifested no clear aggressive intent toward any country, least of all the United States.

Closely related was the argument that the United States had to make war against Iraq, with or without international approval, in order to uphold international law. This argument presumably derived from the idea that Iraq posed a threat, because technical infringements of Security Council resolutions, in the absence of a meaningful threat, are hardly a sufficient justification for the death and destruction that war entails.

A second class of argument was heavily touted by lesser neoconservative figures, but largely unused by Bush and other high officials until a few weeks before the advent of the war. This was the argument that the war was to "liberate" Iraq—an argument belonging to the larger ideology of "humanitarian intervention," which has played such a major role since the early '90s. In this case, war was justified because the United States would bring democracy to Iraq, end the egregious human rights violations committed internally by the Iraqi government, and even, in a particularly clever (and hypocritical) twist, bring an end to the suffering caused by the sanctions. Several ideologues, particularly Richard Perle and Paul Wolfowitz, also fit this into a much more grandiose vision of America as a powerful force for good in the world, in particular a vision of using the "war on terrorism" to bring democracy to the entire Middle East, forcing out dictatorial and religious fundamentalist regimes and replacing them with tolerant Western pluralist democracies that will be natural allies and supporters of "U.S. interests."

With the almost complete collapse of the first category of arguments, the claim of "liberation" has loomed very large in the public debate. Indeed, most mainstream opposition to the neoconservative program is of the "Arabs aren't ready for democracy kind," not the kind that questions U.S. motives.

The reason is that so much of the debate over war has been cut off from the history of U.S. policy toward Iraq and toward the Middle East. For example, many in the antiwar movement touted "containment"–sanctions, inspections, and "no-fly zones"—as the alternative to the war. This even though "containment" was far more deadly in the overall loss of lives than the three weeks of American warfare in the spring of 2003.

This section begins with a thorough review of containment, continues with an analysis of the "pre-emption doctrine," analyzes both categories of arguments laid out above, and concludes with a discussion of what has always been the primary driving force behind U.S. policy in the region—not liberation, but control of oil as a crucial component of global hegemony.

CHAPTER 4

Understanding "Containment"

Iraq after the Gulf War–Sanctions, No-Fly Zones,
and Weapons Inspections

IN THE MONTHS LEADING up to the war on Iraq, perhaps the most common anti-war argument was that "containment has worked." In analogy with the policy of "containment" of communism by the United States during the Cold War,[68] the term has often been used to describe the policies imposed on Iraq after the Gulf War, some by the United Nations and some by the United States, and maintained for over a decade primarily by the will of the United States. The term is intended to suggest that the policy is a defensive one designed to guard against the threat posed by Iraq (just like the perpetual claim that the Cold War was about U.S. defense against Soviet aggression), and perhaps also to imply that it is a relatively benign, non-destructive policy.

AFTER THE WAR

On August 6, 1990, within days after Iraq invaded Kuwait, the United States shepherded the passage of U.N. Security Council Resolution (UNSCR) 661, which imposed comprehensive sanctions on Iraq until it withdrew from Kuwait. Unprecedented in their scope and severity, the sanctions prohibited all exports and all imports, with medicines the only exemption (shortly thereafter, UNSCR 666 exempted food imports from the ban). Any imports had to be approved by the Sanctions Committee, which had one representative from each nation on the Security Council, and any member of which could veto a contract for any reason. Resolution 665, in turn, provided for enforcement by creation of a U.S.-led international naval blockade.

The sanctions hit particularly hard because Iraq's economy was built around the export of oil as the dominant income source, and use of the money earned to import essential goods—before the invasion, Iraq had bought roughly 70 percent of its food and even more of its medicine from abroad.[69]

Although in theory, food was exempted from the sanctions, in practice the sanctions were little more than an attempt to influence Iraqi policy by starving the people. For example, between August 6, 1990, and April 1991, Iraq was able to import roughly 10,000 tons of grain—the equivalent of Iraq's *daily* grain import requirement before the invasion of Kuwait. At one time, the United States even blocked a contract to import baby food from Bulgaria because, said the U.S. representative on the Sanctions Committee, adults might eat it.[70]

Iraq lost the Gulf War, but because of developments we'll discuss later, Saddam Hussein remained in power. This enabled the re-imposition of sanctions and, in fact, allowed the United States to retain tremendous leverage over Iraq, mostly through the medium of the U.N. Security Council. Had any regime not associated with Hussein's crimes (in particular, the invasion of Kuwait) succeeded to power, mustering international support for "containment" would have been, at the least, far more difficult, and maintaining it for 12 years likely impossible.

UNSCR 687 AND WEAPONS OF MASS DESTRUCTION

The initial mechanism for containment was U.N. Security Council Resolution 687, passed in April 1991. Its provisions were modified and supplemented by subsequent resolutions, but much of the framework it created remained intact until the war.

An omnibus resolution dubbed by many the "Mother of all Resolutions," 687 centers on two concepts: sanctions, as discussed above, and weapons of mass destruction (WMD), a catchall rubric for biological, chemical, and nuclear weapons. Always a significant theme in U.S. foreign policy, WMD took on a major propaganda role before the Gulf War.

As the first Bush administration scrambled to find a way to sell the war to the American people, various trial balloons were floated—restoring the "legitimate" government of Kuwait, upholding the rule of law, protecting access to oil. The American public deemed none of these sufficient to justify a large-scale military conflict. Secretary of State James Baker hit a particularly low note when he said, "To bring it down to the level of the average American citizen, let me say that means jobs. If you want to sum it up in one word, it's jobs."[71] Although this nicely epitomized both the brute utilitarianism and the patrician arrogance of the first Bush administration, it simply confused people.

The one *casus belli* that a majority of the American public consistently accepted was the threat that Iraq might develop nuclear weapons in the near future.

Thus, UNSCR 687 required the "destruction, removal, or rendering harmless, under international supervision," of all Iraq's biological and chemical weapons and ballistic missiles with a range greater than 150 kilometers (these being of significance primarily as potential delivery vehicles for WMD warheads), as well as parts and facilities necessary to their manufacture; it also mandated that Iraq not acquire nuclear weapons or necessary components thereof. It created the U.N. Special Commission (UNSCOM), which shared responsibility along with the International Atomic Energy Agency for on-site inspection of Iraqi facilities (the IAEA overseeing the nuclear facilities) as part of monitoring and verification of Iraqi disarmament.

The sanctions, including restrictions on the importation of anything but food, medicine, and "essential civilian needs" and a ban on exports, were to remain in force until Iraq was certified by UNSCOM and the IAEA as clean with regard to all proscribed categories of weapons. Unfortunately, the resolution was somewhat ambiguous; although Paragraph 22 does clearly state that disarmament would lead to lifting of the sanctions, Paragraph 21 says that review of the sanctions will be done "in the light of the policies and practices of the Government of Iraq." The United States and United Kingdom consistently interpreted, or claimed to interpret, this paragraph as giving them leeway to impose whatever demands they saw fit.

WEAPONS INSPECTIONS 1991-1998

The impression of weapons inspections fostered by the Bush administration and much of the press was one of a Keystone Cops affair, with hapless inspectors seriously making their rounds while gloating Iraqis smuggled everything incriminating out the back, returning it all once the inspectors were gone. In this official version, inspections didn't work because they required Iraqi cooperation, which was not forthcoming, and finally broke down completely when Iraq "expelled" the inspectors in December 1998—in some variants, this expulsion is what triggered the Desert Fox bombing campaign of that same month.[72]

The truth is rather different, but one must begin with the recognition that Iraq did indeed do its best to reveal as little as possible of its programs and consistently tried to use partial compliance as a bargaining chip. Inspections started in early June of 1991 and by June 23, Iraqi officials had held up at gunpoint inspectors trying to intercept Iraqi vehicles taking Calutrons (nuclear-related equipment) out of an inspection site. In March 1992 Iraq admitted that it had concealed the existence of 89 ballistic missiles and some chemical weapons, but claimed to have destroyed them unilaterally in the summer of 1991. This unilateral destruction persisted as an issue; toward the end, the main inspection effort was not to find weapons but simply to find documentation so that claims of destruction could be verified.

When UNSCR 715, setting forth modalities for Ongoing Monitoring and Verification, was passed in October 1991, Iraq refused to accept its provisions for more than two years. In fall 1997, Iraq prevented UNSCOM from inspecting several sites on the basis that they were "presidential sites" associated with national sovereignty and the security of the head of state, not with disarmament. In general, as new discoveries were made, Iraq repeatedly amended earlier "Full, Final, and Complete" disclosures. Numerous Security Council resolutions were passed requiring Iraq, under threat of force, to start complying.

This partial lack of cooperation did not, however, make it impossible for inspectors to do their job. Inspectors had broad powers not only to visit sites but to take soil and atmospheric samples and access surveillance photos and other information accumulated by other nations' intelligence agencies, including those of the United States. Of the three kinds of WMD, nuclear weapons programs are easiest to detect because of the radiation involved; chemical weapons are next, because the chemicals involved can often be detected from area sampling. Biological agents can easily be hidden in someone's freezer, but facilities to weaponize biological agents are much harder to hide—and effective weaponization is very difficult.

So, for example, in July 1995 Iraq was compelled to admit the existence of an offensive biological weapons program. This admission is often misrepresented as being a consequence of the defection of Hussein Kamel, Hussein's son-in-law and minister of industry and minerals, not of inspections, but this defection occurred in August 1995, so could hardly have caused an event that happened a month earlier.

According to the March 1999 Amorim report[73] prepared for the Security Council, the achievements of UNSCOM and the IAEA included, but were not limited to, removal of all "weapon usable nuclear material" by February 1994; destruction of all or nearly all imported missiles, missile launchers, chemical and biological warheads; destruction of over 88,000 chemical munitions, nearly 5,000 tons of chemical weapon agents and precursor chemicals; and destruction of al-Hakam, the main biological weapons production complex, along with much biological growth media and equipment. Although there were some unresolved issues regarding some weapons of minor destructive capacity, like 550 mustard-gas-filled artillery shells that Iraq claimed were lost after the Gulf War, the report concluded: "Although important elements still have to be resolved, the bulk of Iraq's proscribed weapons programmes has been eliminated."

Indeed, according to former weapons inspector Scott Ritter, speaking in the fall of 2002, "The primary problem at this point is one of accounting. Iraq has destroyed 90–95 percent of its weapons of mass destruction. Okay. We have to remember that this missing 5-10 percent doesn't necessarily constitute a threat. It doesn't even constitute a weapons program."[74] As of the termination of inspections, according to Ritter, "Iraq presented a WMD-based threat to no one."[75]

So despite incomplete Iraqi cooperation, UNSCOM inspectors did the lion's share of what they had to do, with mostly technical issues remaining to be resolved. Next, we must consider the actual reasons that weapons inspections broke down.

From the beginning, the United States tried to make sure that there was no road map pointing to a clear end of "containment." U.S. policy has often been conceptualized as "moving goalposts," but, in fact, there never were any goalposts. The refusal to specify what actions would be sufficient to merit lifting of sanctions, combined with an "all stick and no carrot" approach in which there were no rewards for partial Iraqi compliance, gave Iraq no incentive to comply fully with disarmament requirements.

The general belief implicit in the American public dialogue has always been that had the government of Iraq simply complied, sanctions would have been lifted—a remarkable belief considering the repeated public statements by U.S. government officials to the contrary. For example, on May 20, 1991, seven weeks after passage of UNSCR 687, James Baker said, "We are not interested in seeing a relaxation of sanctions as long as Saddam Hussein is in power."[76] In 1994, Secretary of State Warren Christopher wrote in a *New York Times* op-ed, "The U.S. does not believe that Iraq's compliance with Paragraph 22 of Resolution 687 is enough to justify lifting the embargo."[77] Perhaps most damaging because of its timing was then Secretary of State Madeleine Albright's statement on March 26, 1997, that "we do not agree with the nations who argue that if Iraq complies with its obligations concerning weapons of mass destruction, sanctions should be lifted. Our view, which is unshakable, is that Iraq must prove its peaceful intentions... And the evidence is overwhelming that Saddam Hussein's intentions will never be peaceful."

The inspections regime started to break down in 1997 and 1998, as Iraq grew tired of the lack of progress on sanctions (the breakdown is covered at greater length in Milan Rai's excellent book *War Plan Iraq*).

A crisis was narrowly averted in February 1998 when U.N. Secretary General Kofi Annan flew to Baghdad to obtain an agreement on inspecting so-called "presidential sites," something the Iraqis had been trying to prevent.

In August, frustrated with the lack of progress on sanctions (in particular, by its inability to sell oil), Iraq decided to stop cooperating with inspections until its concerns were addressed, although it allowed monitoring to continue. Shortly thereafter, Kofi Annan undertook a comprehensive review of the sanctions, in which he considered partly shifting the burden of proof onto the inspectors and also setting some kind of reasonable timetable for ending the sanctions.[78]

Then, on October 30, the Security Council sent a letter that undermined these attempted reforms; in particular, the council, "omitted the guarantee that Iraq would be released from sanctions on a certain date."[79] On October 31, likely assuming that the sanctions would continue forever, Iraq decided to halt all UNSCOM operations in Iraq.

This breakdown of cooperation is usually claimed by

official U.S. sources to be entirely Iraq's fault. *The Financial Times*, on the other hand, clearly stated at the time that "Mr. Saddam's [sic] decision to cripple UNSCOM was triggered by the U.S. refusal explicitly to commit itself to lifting the oil embargo if Iraq complied with disarmament requirements."[80]

After this breakdown, under threat of attack, Iraq resumed cooperation on November 14, 1998. In the next month, over 300 inspections were conducted; UNSCOM head Richard Butler's report, delivered to the Security Council on December 15, cited only five relatively minor problematic incidents. Somehow, entirely belying his own report, he concluded that "no progress" had been made.[81]

Bill Clinton saw the initial draft ahead of time and declared it to be too weak. The next day, according to the *Washington Post*, U.S. government officials played "a direct role in shaping Butler's text during multiple conversations with him at secure facilities at the U.S. mission to the United Nations." On December 15, on the "advice" of U.S. Ambassador to the U.N. Peter Burleigh, Butler recalled inspectors without notifying the Security Council—in explicit violation of a promise he had made to the Security Council after an earlier withdrawal.[82] The conclusion that Butler colluded with the United States to help provide some justification, no matter how thin, for Desert Fox is inescapable.

Another concern claimed frequently by the Iraqis was

that inspections were a cover for U.S. spying. Shortly after the Desert Fox bombings, such allegations were confirmed when the *Washington Post* revealed that "the United States for nearly three years intermittently monitored the coded radio communications of President Saddam Hussein's innermost security forces using equipment secretly installed in Iraq by U.N. weapons inspectors."[83]

The conduct of Desert Fox confirms the intent of said monitoring. Billed as an operation to "degrade" Iraq's weapons-making capacity (utterly foolish because inspections were accomplishing far more than any bombings could, and it was known that inspectors would likely not be allowed back into Iraq after the bombings), it was actually aimed at "regime targets." Of 97 sites targeted in Desert Fox, only 11 were associated with WMD. The vast majority were command and control sites, Republican Guard units, and key facilities of internal security forces.[84]

The operation, planned for at least a year in advance, was an attack on the regime, attempting to make use of the intelligence acquired by the aforementioned espionage before that information became "stale." During the year of planning, the United States frequently directed inspectors to behave in ways that would create provocations.

In 2002, in an interview on Swedish radio, Rolf Ekeus, head of UNSCOM from 1991 to 1997, confirmed all these conclusions. The *Financial Times* reported:

[Mr. Ekeus said] As time went on, some countries, especially the U.S., wanted to learn more about other parts of Iraq's capacity.

Mr. Ekeus said the U.S. tried to find information about the whereabouts of Saddam Hussein, Iraq's president. He said he was able to rebuff such moves but that the pressure mounted after he left in 1997.

Most damning, he said that the U.S. and other members of the Security Council pressed the teams to inspect sensitive areas, such as Iraq's ministry of defence, when it was politically favourable for them to create a crisis situation. 'They [Security Council members] pressed the inspection leadership to carry out inspections which were controversial from the Iraqis' view, and thereby created a blockage that could be used as a justification for a direct military action,' he said.[85]

Far from being concerned with disarming Iraq, the United States deliberately undermined a largely successful inspections regime by eliminating Iraq's incentive (the lifting of sanctions); manipulating the inspections to create political incidents; illicit espionage; and, finally, removal of the inspectors in order to achieve "regime change" through massive bombing and invasion.

SANCTIONS

> *I am willing to make a bet to anyone here that we care more about the Iraqi people than Saddam Hussein does.*
> —Then U.S. Secretary of State Madeleine Albright, CNN Town Hall Meeting, Columbus, Ohio, February 18, 1998

> *We have heard that a half million children have died. I mean, that's more children than died in Hiroshima. And, you know, is the price worth it?*
> —Lesley Stahl on U.N. sanctions against Iraq, *60 Minutes*, May 12, 1996

> *I think this is a very hard choice, but the price—we think the price is worth it.*—Then U.S. Ambassador to the U.N. Madeleine Albright, replying

While inspections continued, a far more compelling and significant drama was playing out—the progressive deterioration and destruction of an entire society.

The mainstream U.S. discourse about sanctions on Iraq has generally oscillated between the two poles marked out by the above statements of Madeleine Albright—a hard-nosed assessment that U.S. policy objectives are more important than the deaths of children (rarely so honestly stated), and sanctimony about the great U.S. government concern for the Iraqi people combined with crocodile tears about Saddam Hussein's cruelty (which few people contest). Just as the big question with regard to inspections was "Why doesn't he just cooperate and get sanctions lifted," the big questions regarding sanctions include "Why did he wait so long before agreeing to the Oil for Food program?" and "Why did he spend the money on palaces and weapons instead of feeding his people?"

Let's start by noting that the term "sanctions" is itself highly misleading. The United States has levied unilateral sanctions on hundreds of occasions. The United Nations has authorized sanctions on 14 different occasions. Never, however, have there been such comprehensive international restrictions on all exports and imports; never have prohibitions on imports been enforced by attaching a country's entire foreign earnings and placing them in a closely monitored bank account, with numerous bureaucratic impediments to disbursement of funds. The confusion engendered by the term is exemplified in a particularly fatuous statement by Marc Cooper, one of an emerging group of self-appointed spokespeople for the antiwar movement. In an article lamenting the stupidity of said movement, he suggests that the Left "must get its story straight on sanctions"—how can it oppose those on Iraq when "the entire American Left supported similar painful sanctions against the apartheid state of South Africa?"[86]

Of course, in South Africa, the African National Congress, the mass movement representing those that would be hardest hit by sanctions, called for them.[87] But even more important are the dramatic differences in the actual sanctions: Just imagine the response had anyone suggested that South Africa be ringed by a naval blockade, that it be denied the right to export anything for years and when it did, that all its foreign earnings be seized and held, with disbursement of funds for medicine and essential civilian infrastructure like water treatment regularly blocked or delayed, and that all this be done after the country had been bombed into rubble.

When you've got the story straight, the sanctions on Iraq emerge as one of the worst horrors of our time.

BRIEF HISTORICAL REVIEW OF THE SANCTIONS

Within months after the end of the Gulf War, numerous reports indicated a catastrophe in the making. In April, the Harvard Study Team, a group of doctors and social scientists, predicted that unless something was done, "at least 170,000 children under five years of age will die in the coming year from the delayed effects of the Gulf Crisis." A similar report issued in March by U.N. Undersecretary General Martti Ahtisaari said that the Gulf War had inflicted "near-apocalyptic results," and predicted "imminent catastrophe."[88]

By 1994, with its industrial base in ruins and devoid of any outside income, Iraq was in the grip of widespread, severe malnutrition. In 1996, the Oil for Food (OFF) program was instituted. Initially, it allowed Iraq to sell $4 billion worth of oil per year. Later, the cap on sales was raised to $10.5 billion and in December 1999 eliminated entirely. Of that money, initially 30 percent and more recently 25 percent was taken for the U.N. Compensation Fund, intended to compensate victims of Iraq's invasion of Kuwait. Its largest beneficiaries have been oil companies, including the Kuwait Petroleum Company, which was awarded damages of $15.9 billion. Another 3 to 4 percent went for U.N. administrative expenses, including those of the weapons inspectors.

All of the money Iraq got for selling its oil through the program was deposited in a bank account in New York, and funds were only disbursed to meet contracts with foreign corporations that were approved by the Sanctions Committee, each member of which could delay or put on hold any contract, without giving any reason. The situation improved only with the passage in May 2002 of UNSCR 1409, which allowed for all goods except those on a special Goods Review List to be automatically approved.

Oil for Food goods started entering Iraq in March 1997. As of February 21, 2003, $43 billion worth of goods had been approved for import, but only $26.6 billion had actually entered Iraq through the program. Between March 1997 and January 2002, the average rate of entry of goods was about $14-15 per month per person, and since then it has only been roughly double that.

Needless to say, this was never enough. In May 1997, UNICEF released a finding, based on studies of 15,000 Iraqi children, that 27.5 percent of children were malnourished, noting that if the condition persists past the age of two, effects are "difficult to reverse" and "damage to the child's development is likely to be permanent."[89] Over the course of the sanctions, adult literacy declined from 80 percent to 58 percent[90] and child literacy similarly—something seen in no other country during the '90s, not even the countries of sub-Saharan Africa being ravaged by AIDS.

Numerous estimates of child deaths due to sanctions have been made, but by far the most authoritative study—and the only one involving independent new data—was done by UNICEF in 1999.[91] Based on a survey of nearly 24,000 households, it concluded that for central and south Iraq the under-age-5 mortality rate, averaged 56 out of 1000 in the period 1984–89 and 131 out of 1,000 from 1994–99—an increase of over 130 percent.[92] Comparing mortality during the sanctions with an extrapolated trend line, it estimated 500,000 excess deaths of children under the age of five during 1991–98. It was careful not to attribute all of them to sanctions. However, the devastation caused by the Gulf War and the sanctions, regarded as a unit, must necessarily account for the vast majority of those deaths; they are the primary things that changed between the 1980s and the 1990s.

The usual response from the U.S. government when confronted with these numbers is both to deny the numbers and to claim that the deaths are Saddam Hussein's fault.

Some of the claims are transparent falsehoods, like the

one that billions in Oil for Food (OFF) funds were diverted to military purchases (not possible because the money never entered Iraq, but was disbursed only for approved purchases). Another problem constantly cited was the president's building of palaces and mosques. Although Hussein's extravagance was never in doubt, again, OFF money simply could not be used for this; furthermore, the total expenditure involved was minuscule as a percentage of national income.

Another objection, which has some merit, is that at times Iraq spent a great deal of money on sophisticated medical equipment (like MRI machines) to provide high-quality care to the wealthy while government hospitals were pitifully short of needles, antibiotics, and other basic goods. It's true that the OFF money could at least theoretically be better spent, not by the huge margin that proponents of the sanctions like to suggest, but certainly significantly. Still, this objection rings very false.

The proponents of massive economic inequality, who have ushered in what the economist Paul Krugman called a new Gilded Age in the United States as well as a rising tide of global economic inequality (a 30-to-1 disparity between the richest 20 percent and the poorest 20 percent globally in 1960 had become a 74-to-1 disparity by 1997), somehow expected complete equality of allocation in Iraq alone—even as, in other countries, their policies have consistently been directed toward increasing inequality of every kind. A country where by deliberate policy 41 million people, disproportionately children, are uninsured and lack sufficient access to basic preventative health care can hardly fault Iraq on the inequality of its allocations. Somehow, Iraq managed to make the champions of the free market discover socialism.

Although the government of Iraq shared some blame, it also deserved some credit. Widespread starvation was averted by institution of a massive food distribution program of nearly unparalleled scope, in which weekly rations were distributed almost for free. Described as "second to none" by Tun Myat, U.N. humanitarian coordinator in Iraq from 2000 to 2002, it never failed to garner high praise from observers.

Of course, the issue of credit for the Iraqi government, which was, after all, a harsh and brutal one, is less fundamental than the question of blame for the United States; how much of the destruction caused by sanctions can be laid at the door of U.S. policy?

OIL FOR FOOD

Perhaps the most notable thing about the sanctions is the long delay before allowing Iraq to sell oil, its only significant source of external income: four years until passage of UNSCR 986, five until Iraq accepted it, five and a half until oil sales started. Since the United States was seemingly willing to allow some oil sales from as early as August 15, 1991, with passage of UNSCR 706, it seems as if the blame for the delay rests entirely on Saddam Hussein, who was content to watch his people starve for years while he asserted his prerogatives.

Actually, the story is somewhat different.

In July 1991, Sadruddin Aga Khan, sent to Iraq by the U.N. Secretary General, estimated that it would cost $22 billion to restore basic sectors in Iraq to prewar levels. Since this represented far more oil than Iraq would likely be allowed to sell, he prepared a minimum estimate of $6.9 billion for full restoration of health and agriculture, half of electrical power, 40 percent of water and sanitation, provision of bare subsistence level amounts of food, and limited repairs to northern oil facilities. He then suggested that Iraq be allowed to sell $2.65 billion worth of oil over four months, with permission to be renewed if no problems emerged.[93]

When this proposal was discussed in the Security Council, the United States caused the period to be lengthened to six months, reduced the amount to $1.6 billion, and required that 30 percent of that be taken for the U.N. Compensation Fund. All told, when the proposal finally passed, the amount to be available for humanitarian needs would have been $930 million for six months—per month, 23 percent of what the Aga Khan had suggested as a minimum, rock-bottom figure.

Thus, it's no surprise that the Iraqi government turned down this measure which would have minimal benefit for its population, bind it to numerous conditions entailing major potentially harmful consequences in the long run, and reduce political pressure for approving higher oil sales. In fact, an aid agency staff member who observed the process said that within weeks of the issuance of the Aga Khan's report, "U.N. officials were convinced ... that the intention was to present Saddam Hussein with so unattractive a package that Iraq would reject it and thus take on the blame, at least in Western eyes, for continuing civilian suffering."[94]

By the end of 1994, with minimal money available, the government announced a 37 percent cut in the food ration, which went below 1,100 calories per person per day—starvation level.[95] As conditions worsened through 1995, Iraq was finally forced to accept Resolution 986, which allowed for $2 billion in sales every six months. Iraq had been forced to capitulate, accepting significant infringement of its sovereignty and what was to turn out to be a crippling way of running its economy in return for a wholly inadequate level of oil sales.

In the end, the United States accepted the resolution only because international political pressure would have made retaining the sanctions untenable otherwise—as Clinton administration official Robert Pelletreau said to a skeptical congressional committee at the time, "Implementation of the resolution is not a precursor to lifting sanctions. It is a humanitarian exception that preserves and even reinforces the sanctions regime."[96]

One can still hold that the Iraqi government should have accepted the very poor deal offered earlier, because the humanitarian crisis was acute and other concerns were longer-range. To claim, however, like Madeleine Albright, that the United States had a greater level of humanitarian concern for Iraqis than did the Iraqi government is simply a shameful distortion of the truth.

HOLDS

Nothing shows the United States' politicization of humanitarian questions and lack of concern for the people of Iraq better than its history of holds, delays, and vetoes. In what follows, I draw heavily from an article by Joy Gordon, published in *Harper's* in November 2002.

In UNSCR 687 itself, although Iraq's possession of conventional military equipment is not proscribed, all imports of military equipment are. Theoretically, potential "dual-use" goods that can have either a civilian or military use are to be handled with care, with their end uses monitored; in practice, the United States simply banned most dual-use items, and construed their definition rather broadly. For most of the duration of the sanctions, the United States followed an unwritten policy of banning goods that were inputs to industry, necessary for revival of the Iraqi economy, but allowing entrance of finished goods for consumption—a fairly typical colonial pattern of economic relationships.[97]

Gordon's investigations span the length of the sanctions and involve numerous sources close to the process; they have led her to the conclusion that "The United States has fought aggressively throughout the last decade to purposefully minimize the humanitarian goods that enter the country."[98]

The United States imposed well over 1,000 holds on contracts, followed by Britain with over 100. According to Gordon:

> In early 2001, the United States had placed holds on $280 million in medical supplies, including vaccines to treat infant hepatitis, tetanus, and diphtheria, as well as incubators and cardiac equipment.
>
> The rationale was that the vaccines contained live cultures, albeit highly weakened ones. The Iraqi government, it was argued, could conceivably extract these, and eventually grow a virulent fatal strain, then develop a missile or other delivery system that could effectively disseminate it.
>
> UNICEF and U.N. health agencies, along with other Security Council members, objected strenuously. European biological-weapons experts maintained that such a feat was in fact flatly impossible. At the same time, with massive epidemics ravaging the country, and sky-

rocketing child mortality, it was quite certain that preventing child vaccines from entering Iraq would result in large numbers of child and infant deaths.[99]

The United States relented only after the *Washington Post* ran a story on the situation. But subsequently, on December 30, 2002, with passage of UNSCR 1454, the United States once again had several basic antibiotics, including streptomycin, added to the Goods Review List if they were contracted for in quantities that "exceed the established consumption rates." Such medicines had already been in perilously short supply in Iraq.

Another problem occurred so frequently that it was given a special name: "complementarity." The United States would selectively approve contracts in such a way that Iraq got insulin without syringes, blood bags without catheters—even a sewage treatment plant without the generator needed to run it.[100] Against its will, Iraq ended up wasting money on useless goods, which then piled up in warehouses, leading to the omnipresent claims that the Iraqi government was "hoarding" its goods.

Holds were also used to target entire infrastructure sectors. According to Gordon, most contracts pertaining to electrical power generation and telecommunications were blocked by the United States.

Potable water was perhaps the single biggest humanitarian concern since the late '90s (as food was during the first several years of the sanctions). By 1996, Iraq's previously excellent sewage treatment system had completely broken down. This was due to damage from the Gulf War (including the systematic bombing of all electrical power, which caused water treatment to shut down), and then to Iraq's inability to fix the system under sanctions. After five years of Oil for Food, UNICEF found that access to potable water had scarcely improved "and "specifically cited the half-billion dollars of water-and sanitation-supply contracts then blocked—one third of all submitted."[101]

The United States cannot even claim ignorance of the likely effects of keeping Iraq from fixing its water treatment facilities. A number of declassified documents, including a Defense Intelligence Agency report entitled "Iraq Water Treatment Vulnerabilities" that was circulated to all allied commands the day after bombing started in 1991, show that the strain on Iraq's water system and the concomitant explosion of waterborne disease was explicitly anticipated.[102]

Holds were also explicitly politicized. In June 2001, when the United States was pushing an early version of its "smart sanctions" proposal (a very different and watered-down form of which was eventually encapsulated in UNSCR 1409), it suddenly lifted $800 million in holds, $200 million of which involved key Security Council members. To court China, a few weeks later it unblocked $80 million in Chinese contracts, including some that had been blocked for dual-use concerns. After

Russia indicated that it would veto the draft resolution, "the United States placed holds on nearly every contract that Iraq had with Russian companies."[103] Such behavior makes a mockery of the claim that holds had to do with security concerns. The Iraqi people suffered directly as a result of the political games that the United States played.

THE SANCTIONS AND IRAQI SOCIAL STRUCTURE

The United States, in its partial administration of Iraq through the sanctions, oversaw a decline in literacy, as elementary schools emptied for lack of supplies and Iraq was forced to impose user fees. It saw the near-total destruction of the middle class and a massive "brain drain," as doctors, scientists, engineers, and other socially necessary people fled to the West. Iraqi society reconstructed along typical Third World lines, with the evolution of a phenomenally corrupt and fabulously opulent elite while people begged for bread in the streets.

While it is true that Saddam Hussein built palaces and cared more for maintaining his power and his military than for the well-being of the Iraqi people, the United States knew this well while it supported him in the 1980s. The sanctions by design threw the Iraqi people to the mercy of the government because the local economy was devastated and all necessary goods came via the government. The United States has never explained the logic behind inflicting suffering on Iraqis to get Saddam Hussein to change his policies while simultaneously claiming that he didn't care about that suffering. It was an overt recipe for a stalemate, while people starved and died.

The sanctions on Iraq were a form of economic control far beyond the dreams of the average IMF economist (though they talk about "free markets," what they want is countries whose economies they can tightly control for the benefit of foreign corporations). Other countries are pressured to cut government payrolls. Iraq's oil earnings were simply seized and put in a foreign bank account so they couldn't be used to pay government salaries. Other countries are encouraged to buy from foreign corporations (through lowering of tariffs and other measures)—Iraq's oil earnings could *only* be used to buy from foreign corporations, or they sat in the bank, untouchable by Iraq.

This external control of Iraq's oil money meant a complete collapse of the country's economy—the government could not hire local contractors or pay salaries with the oil money, and there was virtually nothing available for any kind of investment. The government also had to pay high prices for foreign food rather than buying from Iraqi food producers, causing a drain on its funds and destroying agricultural markets.

These fundamental structural problems persisted even as formal restrictions on goods were relaxed—first with the passage of UNSCR 1284 in December 1999, which mandated the creation of "green lists" of items that would automatically be approved for import and later with the passage of UNSCR 1409 in May 2002, which made all approval automatic except for items on a special proscribed "red list." To borrow a phrase used by the *Economist* about an earlier "smart sanctions" proposal, those resolutions were "an aspirin where surgery is called for."[104]

As Kofi Annan has reported, Oil-for-food was "never intended...to be a substitute for normal economic activity."[105] And, according to Human Rights Watch, "an emergency commodity assistance programme like oil-for-food, no matter how well funded or well run, cannot reverse the devastating consequences of war and then ten years of virtual shut-down of Iraq's economy."[106]

In addition to the destruction of normal economic functioning under the sanctions, the centralized purchase and distribution of a whole society's needs imposed a burden that the Iraqi bureaucracy could not bear. In 2000 and 2001, when larger amounts of money were coming into the OFF program, the secretary general reported that "with the increased funding level and the growing magnitude and scope of the programme, the whole tedious and time-consuming process of the preparation and approval of the distribution plan and its annexes are no longer in step with current realities."[107]

The sanctions also caused a complete collapse of Iraq's currency. The official exchange rate originally maintained by Iraq was .311 dinar to 1 dollar; sanctions caused the actual rate to collapse to 2,000 dinars to 1 dollar by 2002. As a result, long time civil servants were making $5 or $10 per month and even skilled government employees couldn't support themselves without an outside job.

Even leaving aside all of the political manipulation involved in the holds, the external control of Iraq's economy was an evil in itself. It kept the country from being reconstructed by the efforts of its people, and even led to a progressive deterioration in numerous crucial areas. Superficially, nothing could be further apart than the overbearing trade restrictions imposed on Iraq and the "free trade" being imposed on most of the rest of the world at the same time, but in fact the results were very similar because of the crucial shared feature—First World control of, or influence over, a Third World economy.

NO-FLY ZONES AND BOMBINGS

The third component of "containment" was the "no-fly zones" and the frequent bombings associated with them. The United States and United Kingdom jointly patrolled a northern no-fly zone above the 36th parallel in Iraq and a southern one below the 33rd (France pulled out of joint enforcement in 1996). The northern one was imposed in April 1991, largely because of international outrage at the plight of Kurdish refugees in the north—the United States had, as mentioned above, allowed the slaughter of Kurds and generation of millions of refugees with great aplomb until the uncomfortable pictures started to be seen by Western audiences in their living rooms. The southern no-fly zone was not imposed until August 1992, even though the slaughter of the Shia after the Gulf War was no less intense.

The United States often claimed that these zones were authorized by UNSCR 688, but that is transparently false. UNSCR 688 is not a Chapter VII resolution, meaning it does not authorize the use of force, and it makes no mention of no-fly zones—the closest it comes is appealing to member states to contribute to "humanitarian relief efforts." The zones were, in fact, an illegal imposition.

After the Desert Fox bombing campaign, the no-fly zones became the site of frequent confrontations, whereby Iraqi antiaircraft batteries would "illuminate" or occasionally attack American and British fighters, and they in turn would respond with bombs. According to Hans von Sponeck, a former U.N. humanitarian coordinator for Iraq, these bombings killed hundreds of Iraqi civilians, most of them from the groups, Kurds and Shias, that the no-fly zones supposedly protected.

CHAPTER 5

9/11 and the Pre-emption Doctrine
From Box-Cutters to Weapons of Mass Destruction

EVER SINCE THE TOWERS came down, a U.S. war on Iraq was in the cards. The revelation by CBS News in September 2002 that Defense Secretary Rumsfeld had within hours of the attacks sent a memo to aides directing them to find some way to pin the attack on Iraq—"best info fast. Judge whether good enough hit S.H. [Saddam Hussein] at same time. Not only UBL [Usama bin Laden]"—was no revelation at all to those who have studied U.S. policy toward Iraq. Nor was it shocking to find that Rumsfeld was not overly concerned with whether Iraq was actually involved—"Go massive...sweep it all up.... Things related and not."[108]

On the surface, at least, an attack carried out by a stateless terrorist network using box-cutters is not quite *prima facie* evidence that Iraq, or any other U.S.-designated "rogue state," is plotting either to turn over weapons of mass destruction to terrorists or to attack the United States directly. The logical leap, enshrined also in the National Security Strategy, is a large one. A stateless terrorist organization that is undeterrable because direct retaliation is difficult or impossible has very different considerations from a state that is over-whelmingly inferior to the United States militarily and would be devastated by the inevitable military response.

Thus, a lot of fast talking combined with an interest-ing confluence of events and arguments were necessary to make the link in the public consciousness.

The anthrax attacks were a key component of this process. As soon as they occurred, conservative com-mentators seized on them as proof that Iraq was target-ing Americans. Later, it transpired that the origin of the anthrax strain was American and the most plausible conclusion was that the source of the letters was a U.S. government employee, so the issue was quietly dropped. The damage, however, had largely been done—Iraq and the potential bio-terrorist threat it supposedly represented had been resurrected as a pressing issue. The fact that the United States had once developed weapons-grade anthrax and that Americans had died as a result of its own illicit bio-weapons programs was conveniently ignored.[109]

In early November 2001, Undersecretary of State for Arms Control John Bolton built on this with a public accusation that Iraq, along with North Korea, was violating the Biological and Toxin Weapons Convention (BTWC). He then linked this to 9/11 through the device that was to become standard: "We also know that Usama bin Ladin considers obtaining weapons of mass destruction to be a sacred duty...We are concerned that he could have been trying to acquire a rudimentary biological weapons capability, possibly with support from a state."[110] Nowhere is there even implied evidence that any state actually helped al-Qaeda to obtain any weapons of mass destruction. Nor was there any new evidence to prompt this sudden press conference (Iraq's violations had been well known since at least 1995).

In December 2001, the House International Affairs Committee completed the link when it considered a resolution declaring that "the refusal by Iraq to admit United Nations weapons inspectors into any facility covered by the provisions of Security Council Resolution 687 should be considered an act of aggression against the United States and its allies"—remarkable language, considering that "aggression" is usually taken to involve some actual attack. A flurry of Internet-driven activism by the anti-sanctions movement helped prompt the committee to change "act of aggression" to "growing threat," in which form the resolution passed the House by a margin of 393-12.

The stage was set for the introduction of the "pre-emption doctrine."

THE PRE-EMPTION DOCTRINE

Especially in the summer and early fall of 2002, the pre-emption doctrine was the main rhetorical justification for the war on Iraq and also the occasion for an unusual debate among the political elite. Representative Dick Armey (R-Texas), who had shortly before advocated ethnic cleansing of the Palestinians in the occupied territories,[111] opined in August that a war on Iraq in accord with the doctrine would be a violation of international law (although in October, he voted in favor of the resolution for war). Henry Kissinger noted, "It is not in the American national interest to establish pre-emption as a universal principle available to every nation."[112] At one point, even George Bush Sr. seemed to get into the act, with closely spaced criticisms coming from his former secretaries of state James Baker and Lawrence Eagleburger, and his former national security adviser, Brent Scowcroft.

Unfortunately, the debate has obscured far more than it has revealed, with all sides ignoring the larger historical context of U.S. policy. As a result, even the antiwar movement has had a number of misconceptions about this war.

First, some definitions. "Pre-emption" is actually a misnomer, adopted so that the administration could claim that the doctrine has a hallowed history in international law. The term is traditionally used to refer to a situation where an enemy has clearly manifested aggressive intent, has massed its troops, and is obviously just about to attack. In such a case, international law does not require that one wait to be attacked—although it does require that one put the matter before the U.N. Security Council if at all possible before attacking.

The Six-Day War in 1967, which all agree was started by Israel, is often given as an example of legitimate pre-emption because of the supposedly clear and immediate threat posed by Arab armies massing near the borders. The historical record shows clearly it was not—in fact, the Egyptian air force was so unprepared for conflict that it was mostly wiped out on the ground. Imagine, however, a hypothetical case: Suppose there was a huge buildup of U.S. and U.K. troops in the Persian Gulf, a pattern of constant and escalating air strikes on Iraq, a barrage of bellicose rhetoric, and a consistent refusal to negotiate. In such circumstances, an Iraqi attack on those troops might well have been legitimate pre-emption.

When Bush said that we need to attack Iraq because it might have biological or chemical weapons, or it someday might have a nuclear weapon or a delivery system that could reach the United States, even though it had made no moves suggesting an attack on the United States, he was advocating what is usually known as preventive war—i.e., a war to prevent a country from ever acquiring the means to attack one substantially. Since such a justification could easily be used by any country to attack any other, it's long been understood in international legal circles that preventive war is completely illegitimate.

Worse than illegitimate, the doctrine is logically incoherent—as long as one understands it to apply to any country and not to be some special imperial right of the United States. If Country A feels that Country B may attack it pre-emptively, by definition it then has the right to pre-emptively attack Country B in self-defense. By this doctrine, Iraq has a far more secure right to attack the United States than vice versa.

The NSS contains a tortured attempt to justify the doctrine, partly by claiming falsely that it is in accord with widely accepted interpretations of international law, and partly by stating that "the United States has long maintained the option of pre-emptive actions to counter a sufficient threat to our national security."

If one correctly understands "pre-emptive actions" to mean "aggression, against a party that poses little or no threat" and "threat to our national security" to mean "threat to U.S. control or U.S. corporate interests," then this statement is perfectly true.

Discussions of pre-emption have tended to conflate two distinct issues—first, whether or not any given intervention is an act of aggression and second, what are the rhetorical justifications given for intervention.

When Senator Mark Dayton (D-Minn.) wrote in a *Washington Post* opinion piece that "according to researchers at the Library of Congress, the United States has never in its 213-year history launched a pre-emptive attack against another country,"[113] he was clearly fostering the idea that this war is different because all previous U.S. wars were justified responses to attacks by others, but this one is an act of unjustified aggression. Even much of the antiwar movement believes this, that the United States never "shoots first;" this dissociation of Gulf War 2 from the previous history of U.S. foreign policy mirrors an earlier generation's dissociation of Vietnam from that history.

In fact, the war on Iraq was just the latest in a long series of acts of aggression committed by the United States. In most of them, pre-emption has not been the announced justification. In Panama, for example, the claim was that the invasion was self-defense because Panama was a transshipment point (one of many) for drugs entering the United States, which constitutes an attack—a doctrine by which almost any country could attack any other. In Vietnam, the Gulf of Tonkin incident was entirely manufactured and then used as a justification for the war. Other interventions like the CIA coups in Iran and Guatemala were given no justification because they were "covert," but were obviously acts of illegal aggression, with devastating consequences.

The significance of pre-emption lies in the fact that it represents a notable change in rhetoric.

Even the language is not entirely new. The Reagan

administration, for example, claimed that the bombing of Libya in 1986 was "pre-emptive self-defense."

And if we look past the specific terminology, we can see that this doctrine has been prefigured numerous times. In fact, although the official justification for Cold War interventions was the need to contain Communist aggression, one often sees this same logic operating there. When Reagan justified the creation and support of the murderous contras in Nicaragua by pointing out that Nicaragua is only two days' drive from Harlingen, Texas, the only way to interpret it is as follows: There is a long-standing Soviet plot to destroy America militarily; indigenous movements like the Sandinistas are attempts by the Soviets to create forward bases for such an operation; thus, when the United States wrecked the country it was simply defending itself against this tortuously imagined future attack. Absurd as this may seem, it's the way most Cold War interventions were justified to the American public.

Another clear example—of greater present relevance— is the developing strategic doctrine that mere possession of weapons of mass destruction can be justification for war against another country. This is an outgrowth of the standard 1990s strategic shift from a "threat-based" policy, focused on the intentions of other states, to a "capability-based" approach, in which any other state (except, of course, close allies) that has significant military capabilities is automatically classed a threat.[114] Since capability alone reveals nothing about intent, military attacks arising from the previously mentioned "capability-based" approach, and specifically those based on possession or suspected possession of WMD, automatically qualify as preventive war.

Although tried out a few times over the years, this particular concept was seriously launched with the August 1998 bombing of the El Shifa pharmaceutical plant in the Sudan based on claims that it was producing chemical weapon precursors. Then came Desert Fox in December 1998. WMD was the justification given for both attacks, although, as previously discussed, neither was really about WMD.

What's really new about the "pre-emption doctrine" is its explicit codification. One thing this does is do away with the need for the United States to establish or even plausibly to claim aggressive intent on the part of any country before going to war with it. The open abandonment of at least part of the rhetoric of "defense" lays U.S. policy bare to the world, in a way that cannot but provoke opposition.

The codification also has other consequences, of a kind that seriously disquiet the sectors of the U.S. elite that participated in this debate. Perhaps most clearly, as Kissinger pointed out, making pre-emption universal threatens to deprive the United States of its claim to a monopoly on the "legitimate" use of force, which at most it shares with Israel, the U.K., and perhaps a few

Western European countries. If Russia can claim the same right to invade Georgia, or India to invade Pakistan, then the United States is ceding too much of its status as the "only superpower."

Simultaneously, in the case of Iraq, the entire debate over pre-emption was irrelevant for one overwhelming reason—there was no threat to pre-empt.

CHAPTER 6

The Threat from Iraq

BY THE SPRING OF 2003, U.S. claims that a war was necessary because of the threat posed by Iraq had reached ludicrous proportions and included outright lies. One charge that was frequently made, including in the State of the Union address, was that Iraq had attempted to buy uranium from Niger. When the documents on which this claim was based were turned over to the International Atomic Energy Agency, they were immediately spotted as crude forgeries. Errors included putting the wrong name for the Foreign Minister of Niger and referring to an outdated constitution—things that could have been discovered even with a cursory Internet search.[115] Hans Blix, chief weapons inspector, characterized the U.S. government's failure to uncover this forgery as "disturbing."[116]

Among the earlier absurdities was George W. Bush's assertion that Iraq's unmanned aerial vehicles (UAV) presented a threat to the United States even though their range is a few hundred miles, and there is a massive ocean between the United States and Iraq. When the UAV's were finally unveiled, they proved to be little more than children's toys, unable to carry a significant payload.

There were also outright lies and coverups. After Iraq had started destroying its al-Samoud 2 missiles, on March 3, 2003, White House press spokesperson Ari Fleischer said that Hussein "denied he had these weapons, and then he destroys things he says he never had. If he lies about never having them, how can you trust him when he says he has destroyed them?" In fact, Iraq had itself turned over material, on December 7, 2002, that indicated the al-Samoud 2 had exceeded the permitted range of 150 km on 13 of 40 tests.

Later it was revealed that high-profile Iraqi defector Hussein Kamel, Saddam's son-in-law, whose revelations of some secret Iraqi weapons programs were constantly cited as "evidence" that inspections don't work had also told UNSCOM that Iraq had destroyed its weapons. "I ordered destruction of all chemical weapons. All weapons—biological, chemical, missile, nuclear were destroyed," he said in an interview shortly before his death. All that remained, he added, was technical documentation and production molds.[117] Even though one can't be sure he was telling the truth, the fact that the statement was deliberately suppressed, at U.S. insistence, for eight years while other things he said were repeatedly played up as conclusive evidence is fairly damning.

The United States also tried desperately to sabotage the

weapons inspections. Even though Clause 10 of UNSCR 1441, which re-established inspections, requests that member states turn over all relevant information to weapons inspectors, the United States refused until February 5, 2003, to turn over any of its extensive aerial reconnaissance information. After it started providing information, inspectors complained that the United States was sending them on "wild goose chases" and that the information being provided to them was "garbage."[118]

The United States also attempted to undermine inspections by making it very clear that acts of cooperation by Iraq would not stop the drive to war. When Hans Blix issued an ultimatum about destruction of the above-mentioned al-Samoud 2 missiles, the Bush administration immediately stated that dismantling of the missiles, though a necessary condition, would make absolutely no difference. As soon as Iraq agreed to obey Blix's order, George W. Bush immediately countered that Iraqi disarmament was not enough to avert war, and that "regime change" was necessary.[119]

All in all, the prewar policy of the United States tends to show that it did not believe its own hype about Iraq's weapons of mass destruction and was willing to go to any length to distort the truth and to short-circuit alternatives to war.

The fact that Iraq used no weapons of mass destruction against the United States makes it clear that there was no threat.

If there were real concerns about WMD, the conduct of the United States after the "regime change" has been remarkable. The vast majority of sites were left unsecured for weeks, with large numbers of weapons inspectors dispatched to Iraq only in late April, 2003. Given that the regime's collapse made it easier, not harder, for terrorist organizations to gain access to any WMD, one can only conclude again that the Bush administration did not believe its own claims.

Finally, if WMD are found in Iraq (and since the administration has refused to allow U.N. weapons inspectors back in, there will always be good reason to suspect that any "finds" could have been planted) the case that Saddam Hussein continues to threaten the United States will be even further diminished. If Hussein didn't use them under the ultimate threat of "regime change," why would he menace the United States with them in peacetime?

IRAQI INTENT

To evaluate retrospectively the Iraqi threat to "the West," we must divide it into intent and capability— mere possession of weapons has not yet been established to be proof of intent to attack Americans, although a casual watcher of Sunday morning TV shows could be forgiven for thinking otherwise. Here, "intent" means not extrapolated unvoiced desires, but at the very least desire linked to a credible capability.

Leaving aside for the moment the question of Iraq's supposed role in the 9/11 attacks, there was never any evidence of a manifest Iraqi intent to attack American targets.

According to the U.S. State Department's *Patterns of Global Terrorism 2000* report, "The regime has not attempted an anti-Western terrorist attack since its failed plot to assassinate former President Bush in 1993 in Kuwait."[120] Even that claim was torn apart by investigative journalist Seymour Hersh in an article in 1993. The main evidence cited by the U.S. government was that the design of certain bomb trigger components showed conclusively that they were of Iraqi provenance. Hersh, on the other hand, interviewed numerous bomb experts who told him that the components were actually "mass-produced items, commonly used for walkie-talkies and model airplanes and cars."[121] The rest of the case was similarly flimsy.

The claim by author Laurie Mylroie that Iraq was behind the 1993 World Trade Center bombing, largely based on a speculative analysis of the identity of a single person, is not believed even by U.S. government analysts.[122] On the other hand, Saad al-Bazzaz, a high-ranking Iraqi defector, claims that in the 1980s Hussein made an explicit decision not to engage in terrorism against the West.[123]

While Bush constantly proclaimed the existence of a threat from Iraq, his own intelligence people were denying it. CIA Director George Tenet, in a letter to Senate Intelligence Committee Chair Bob Graham, said clearly that "Baghdad for now appears to be drawing a line short of conducting terrorist attacks with conventional or CBW [chemical and biological weapons] against the United States." In fact, pointing to the central weakness in the case for pre-emptive war, he added "Should Saddam conclude that a U.S.-led attack could no longer be deterred, he probably would become much less constrained in adopting terrorist actions."[124]

That latter threat did not eventuate, but had the United States genuinely believed Iraq had significant WMD capabilities, Tenet's assessment should have been a compelling argument against war. In fact, so poor was the case for war on Iraq based on a threat that the Bush administration put unprecedented pressure on government officials, including those in the CIA, FBI, and Department of Energy, to modify, even falsify, reports so that they would back up the administration line. According to Vincent Cannistraro, former CIA head of counterintelligence, "Basically, cooked information is working its way into high-level pronouncements and there's a lot of unhappiness about it in intelligence, especially among analysts at the CIA."[125]

The usual arguments for the existence of an Iraqi intent to attack, beyond vague invocations of Saddam Hussein's desire for revenge after the Gulf War, were Iraq's history of regional aggression and, primarily, Saddam's use of chemical weapons "on his own people." In essence, the case was that since Iraq used chemical weapons on the Kurds in 1988 in the middle of its war with Iran, Iraq was therefore an immediate threat to Americans in 2003 that required a swift and deadly war for "regime change."

In fact, the historical record suggests a strikingly different conclusion. Iraq used chemical weapons in two kinds of circumstances. First, against the Iranian military during the Iran-Iraq war. Second, closely related, against Halabja and a handful of other towns in northern Iraq, at a time when the most prominent Kurdish political organizations, the KDP and PUK, were fighting on the side of Iran. These are war crimes, and the willingness to use chemical weapons against a predominantly civilian target like Halabja is, if possible, even more criminal.

However, the United States fully backed Iraq in the Iran-Iraq war. It rewarded Iraq very early on, in 1982, by removing Iraq from the State Department's list of sponsors of international terrorism and then in 1984 by restoring full diplomatic relations with Iraq. It heavily funded Iraq through the 1980s, with over $5 billion in loan guarantees. It also provided Iraq with over $1.5 billion worth of strategically sensitive exports, including what a Senate committee report called "a veritable witch's brew of biological materials."[126] The United States simultaneously provided arms to Iran, pursuing the dual goals of trying to foment a military coup in that country and of having Iraq and Iran commit maximal mutual destruction (estimates of the number killed in the Iran-Iraq war run from roughly 500,000 to 1 million).[127]

The U.S. government continued to provide aid to Iraq as attacks on Kurdish targets continued and to beat down a motion in Congress to censure Iraq for its actions.[128] Recently declassified U.S. government documents indicate that U.S. intelligence was fully aware that Iraq was the culprit—and, according to Joost Hilterman of Human Rights Watch, "The State Department instructed its diplomats to say that Iran was partly to blame"[129] while avoiding details that could show the story was false. To aid this disinformation effort, the U.S. Army War College issued a report claiming to establish that Iran was behind the attack on Halabja. The United States also made sure the Security Council did not act in a meaningful manner.

In other words, Iraq used its chemical weapons only when it knew it had the full approval of the Number One superpower, and used them only against targets, Kurds and Iranians, that it knew full well the Western powers cared little or nothing about. The third of Hussein's most significant atrocities, the bloody suppression of the Iraqi uprising after the Gulf War, was also done with the material support of the United States.

The invasion of Kuwait, an atrocity of a far lesser scale than the others, is slightly more ambiguous. The United States deliberately gave Hussein a series of signs that it would not oppose Iraqi saber-rattling and even border incursions in northern Kuwait. Those signs included statements by government officials like Ambassador to Iraq April Glaspie, White House press spokesperson Margaret Tutwiler, and Assistant Secretary of State James Kelly that the United States did not feel obligated to defend Kuwait, even that it had "no opinion" on "Arab-Arab border disputes."[130] At the time, the United States was well aware of Iraqi troops massing on the Kuwait border. Hussein may not have fully trusted those signs and may well have realized that taking all of Kuwait was going too far, but he might well have refrained from occupying Kuwait had he not been encouraged.

All of this suggests that Iraq was aware that it could not commit regional aggression without the approval of the superpower. As for attacking the superpower directly, Iraq was, of course even more constrained. When Iraq was under attack in the Gulf War, it made no use of any of its chemical weapons. And, of course, even in Gulf War 2—an invasion for "regime change"—Iraq used no such weapons.

No state will attack a country with thousands of nuclear intercontinental ballistic missiles and a proven record not just of using nuclear weapons but of often threatening their use explicitly, such as against North Vietnam in 1969[131] and before Gulf War 1, and in a generalized way as in the *Nuclear Posture Review*. For Iraq, even giving WMD to terrorists would not get around that basic deterrent for the simple reason that even had the weapons not been traced to Iraq, Iraq would have been assumed to be the culprit.

Those realities did not change on September 11, 2001.

IRAQ, AL-QAEDA, AND 9/11

From the beginning, one of the main gambits in the attempt to "go massive" against Iraq was to claim that it had some alliance with al-Qaeda or that it was involved directly in the 9/11 attacks.

The "logic" was simple—Saudis and Egyptians were involved in the 9/11 attacks, so we should attack Afghanistan, Iraq, and then perhaps Iran, Syria, and Libya. The tactic was straightforward—sling enough mud and assume some will stick. It worked remarkably well: although the Bush administration has produced neither any evidence of such a connection nor even any credible claim that has stood up to scrutiny, yet, according to many polls the majority of Americans believed that Iraq was involved in the attacks.[132]

There were always good commonsense reasons to doubt any link between Iraq and al-Qaeda or other radical Islamist groups. Al-Qaeda sees even the extremely rigid religious constraints imposed on the Saudi people by their regime as far too lax and not in accord with the dictates of Islam. The Ba'ath Party, on the other hand, was originally an aggressively secularist organization. Although the Iraqi regime did turn to use of religion as a unifying factor after the Gulf War, Al-Qaeda and Osama bin Laden always viewed the Ba'ath as infidels. Interestingly, even as the White House constantly claimed Hussein was in league with al-Qaeda, it also issued a report claiming "experts know that Saddam Hussein is a non-religious man from a secular—even atheistic—party."[133]

U.S. government claims of possible connections between Iraq and al-Qaeda have never gotten anywhere. By mid-February 2003, Colin Powell, supposedly the most credible member of the Bush administration, was reduced to claiming that an audiotape of bin Laden—in which he denounced the war on Iraq but also denounced its government as "socialists" and "infidels" who had "lost their legitimacy a long time ago"—was somehow proof that bin Laden had been in collusion with the Iraqi government.[134]

One could assume that Powell would not have stooped so low had there been any real evidence. But let's review a few of the allegations anyway.

First was the claim that 9/11 hijacker and ringleader Mohammed Atta met with Ahmed al-Ani, an Iraqi intelligence official, in Prague in April 2001. Even had it been true, this would have said nothing about Iraqi government involvement in 9/11—the primary task of Iraqi intelligence in Prague and similar places is keeping an eye on Iraqi dissidents and opposition groups. But, in fact, American records show that Atta was in Virginia Beach, Virginia, in early April, when the supposed meeting took place, and Czech president Vaclav Havel has told American officials there is no evidence of any meeting.[135]

The main claim made in an important presentation by Powell before the Security Council on February 5, 2003 concerned Abu Musab al-Zarqawi, a Jordanian militant apparently involved with a group known as Ansar al-Islam in northern Iraq. Al-Zarqawi had no clear connection either with al-Qaeda or the government of Iraq (GOI), but in the administration's twisted logic he somehow provided a connection between them.

The full extent of the connection between al-Zarqawi and the GOI was that he apparently got medical care in a Baghdad hospital, hardly an indication of high-level Iraqi complicity in anti-American terrorist attacks.[136] The head of Ansar al-Islam, Mullah Krekar, denies any connection between Ansar and al-Qaeda.[137] Ansar al-Islam's camps were located in Northern Iraq, in the area under the control of pro-U.S. Kurdish groups and not Saddam Hussein, so their existence could hardly have been a reason to go to war with Iraq.

Almost simultaneous with Powell's claims came word of a classified British intelligence report concluding that there are no links between the GOI and al-Qaeda, in fact that any attempt to create a relationship between them "collapsed because of mistrust and incompatible ideologies."[138] Earlier, the *Washington Post*, citing unnamed "senior European officials," had reported that "intelligence reports indicate that Saddam personally decided against allowing bin Laden and al-Qaeda to use Iraq as a base because he feared they might destabilize his regime."[139] And according to Jean-Louis Bruguiere, a French judge who has spent two decades investigating Islamic and Middle Eastern terrorists, "We have found no evidence of links between Iraq and Al Qaeda. And we are working on 50 cases involving Al Qaeda or radical Islamic cells. I think if there were such links, we would have found them."[140]

At best, the argument for an Iraqi link with al-Qaeda boiled down to Defense Secretary Rumsfeld's famous dictum that "the absence of evidence is not evidence of absence."

GIVING WMD TO TERRORISTS

One major stated concern was always that Iraq would give WMD to unspecified, presumably Islamist, terrorist organizations. As we mentioned earlier, this would not have released Iraq from the threat of retaliation.

Furthermore, Hussein saw chemical weapons as the guarantors of his regime's stability, saving it first from Iran and then from the United States. Giving such potentially potent weapons to a group he couldn't completely control, especially an Islamist group that he would perceive as a threat to his regime, would have been, from his point of view, insane. Richard Butler, former head of UNSCOM, said in testimony before the Senate Foreign

Relations Committee, "I have seen no evidence of Iraq providing [weapons of mass destruction] to non-Iraqi terrorist groups. I suspect that, especially given his psychology and aspirations, Saddam would be reluctant to share with others what he believes to be an indelible source of his own power."[141]

In fact, according to the Australian Strategic Policy Institute, "Saddam Hussein is not the most likely source of WMD for terrorists" (Russia and Pakistan were cited as more likely sources), and even more important, "Iraq's WMD are more likely to find their way into al-Qaeda's hands in the chaos that might follow a U.S. invasion, than under Saddam Hussein's closely-controlled regime."[142] Thus, for someone who was truly concerned about the threat of WMD falling into the hands of stateless terrorist organizations, a war on Iraq would have been the worst possible action to take.

WEAPONS OF MASS DESTRUCTION

Before discussing Iraq's weapons of mass destruction, one should note that the very phrase "weapons of mass destruction" itself represents a propaganda victory for the U.S. government. Battlefield chemical weapons of the kind Iraq has used not only have far less destructive power than a nuclear bomb, they are no more destructive than conventional weapons the United States frequently employs, such as daisy cutters. (The United States also uses chemical weapons, like the 11 million gallons of Agent Orange it sprayed on Vietnam.) Biological weapons are more frightening in terms of their maximum theoretical effect and because effects can so easily spread far beyond the intentions of the users, but they are also extremely difficult to weaponize effectively.

Nobody outside Iraq knew exactly what its arsenal might have been, but we do know that no other country has ever been subject to such longstanding, frequent, and intrusive inspections by inspectors with so much power. We certainly knew more about Iraq's WMD than we did about those of any other country, including the United States.

The best analysis, based on a wide variety of official documents and think-tank studies, of what Iraq might at least potentially have had is "Claims and Evaluations of Iraq's Proscribed Weapons," by Dr. Glen Rangwala of Cambridge University, available on the Web (updated regularly) at http://middleeastreference.org.uk/iraqweapons.html. Sources for most statements below can be found in this document.

The United States has made a wide variety of claims about Iraq's alleged WMD capabilities. Almost all have been refuted, like the claim that high-quality aluminum tubes Iraq imported were for use in centrifuges; the last conclusion of IAEA inspectors said that Iraq's claim that the tubes were for conventional artillery use is most likely true (although their import did constitute a violation of UNSCR 687 and subsequent resolutions). Moreover, numerous claims that production had resumed at various old facilities, like al-Qaim and Tuwaitha (nuclear) or al-Dawra, were flatly disproved by onsite visits.

Some general conclusions can be drawn. Throughout the inspections of 1991–98 (and more recently from November 2002 onward), production of WMD in a clandestine fashion was virtually impossible, and even the U.S. does not claim that it was done. Furthermore, the vast majority of any biological and chemical agents that Iraq might have produced earlier would have degraded—including, most likely, Iraq's anthrax supplies, since there is no evidence it produced the durable dry form, and any botulinum toxin. Mustard agents in artillery shells were a possible exception but, in the quantities unaccounted for, are relatively unimportant.

With regard to biological and chemical agents, the problem was this: Iraq could not completely account for the discrepancies between the amounts it obtained (this figure is known very well, since the primary suppliers were German and American companies) and what it claimed were either used in the Iran-Iraq war, destroyed in the Gulf War attacks, or unilaterally destroyed. Thus, estimates of possible amounts of chemical agents are simply maximum possible discrepancies, not actual knowledge of what Iraq is likely to have. Similarly, estimates for biological agents are based on amounts of growth medium unaccounted for combined with unrealistic projections about continual operation of equipment. In the postwar mop-up operations, it quickly became clear that the inflated numbers regularly being bandied about before the war had no connection with reality.

The fear that the Bush administration most loved to conjure up, of course, was that Iraq might develop a nuclear weapon (even though, as discussed above, it would be unable to effectively use such a weapon on another nation). Repeated claims that if Iraq obtained the fissile material it could have a bomb within six months to a year obscure the fact that obtaining the fissile material is the most difficult part of making a bomb—and the easiest to thwart with effective monitoring. Iraq could not build enrichment facilities without their being detectable by gamma-ray emissions, and attempts to acquire highly enriched uranium or plutonium from other countries are easy to monitor. In fact, if inspections were allowed to continue, predicted Mohammed el-Baradei, "the IAEA expects to be able, within the next few months, barring exceptional circumstances and provided there is sustained proactive cooperation by Iraq, to provide credible assurance that Iraq has no nuclear weapons programme."[143]

With Hans Blix ready to make similar assurances, it became very clear that if disarmament were the goal, the inspections should be given more time. No justification was ever given for the feeble U.S. claim that "time was running out."

U.S. SUBVERSION OF INTERNATIONAL DISARMAMENT

In fact, U.S. policy on weapons of mass destruction around the world has clearly also not had disarmament as the goal. Past "disarmament" efforts by the United States have always centered around the idea that the United States and its closest allies (and a few uncontrollable rivals like China) arrogate to themselves the right to possess weapons of mass destruction (nuclear, chemical, or biological), but that for other states to possess them is deeply immoral.

The Nuclear Nonproliferation Treaty (NPT) explicitly encodes this, designating five countries (the United States, United Kingdom, France, the Soviet Union, and China) as nuclear states and all others as permanently non-nuclear. Article VI of the NPT, however, does clearly state that, in addition to halting "horizontal proliferation," "vertical proliferation" must cease as well, and that the nuclear states must move toward eliminating their arsenals. The United States has consistently ignored Article VI, continuing for over a decade after passage of the NPT to increase the size of its nuclear arsenal; as a result, the treaty lost all credibility and Third World states routinely complained about the double standard encoded in it. In fact, had the United States not first undermined the NPT and then destroyed the Comprehensive Test Ban Treaty, it's quite likely that India, and thus Pakistan, would not be openly nuclear powers today.

The Chemical Weapons Convention is much better. It provides equal treatment for all nations, categorically banning all chemical weapons. It also has an enforcement procedure to make it meaningful—any signatory can demand "challenge inspections" of any other state. The United States did not ratify the convention until 1997, and has committed to destroying its chemical arsenal only by 2008. When the U.S. finally did ratify the convention, it introduced an exception to the inspection clause, making ratification largely meaningless. It also routinely uses and contemplates the use of "non-lethal" chemical agents (which do sometimes kill people) that are banned by the convention. Interestingly, in March 2002, the United States forced the removal of Jose Bustani from his job as head of the Organization for the Prevention of Chemical Wapons because he was trying to include Iraq in the Chemical Weapons Convention (subjecting it to chemical weapons inspections).[144]

The United States has also compromised attempts to control biological weapons through the same kind of double standard. The Biological and Toxin Weapons Convention, promulgated in 1972, signed now by 146 countries, had no enforcement mechanism, so many signatories, including the Soviet Union, Iraq, and almost certainly the United States, violated it. In 1995, countries embarked on a process to develop a comprehensive protocol like that in the CWC, culminating in a draft agreement in 2001. After years of watering down the enforcement mechanism, in part because inspections might compromise proprietary material in the hands of biotech corporations, in July 2001, the United States announced that it could not support such a mechanism, planning instead to rely on espionage, multilateral agreements on export restrictions with allies in the so-called Australia Group, and occasionally unilateral enforcement by military means. In December of the same year, the Bush administration dealt what was likely the final deathblow to the enforcement mechanism.

All of the problems created by these efforts would have been reversible if the United States had been willing to give up or even reduce its own stores of weapons of mass destruction. The war on Iraq, however, has changed all of that; disarmament is impossible for the foreseeable future. In fact, for those countries wishing to make sure the United States doesn't attack them in the future, proliferation is the order of the day.

One of the most absurd moments in a very absurd post-9/11 world came on April 9, 2003, when John Bolton, U.S. undersecretary of state for arms control and international security, used the war on Iraq to warn Iran, Syria, and North Korea: "With respect to the issue of the proliferation of weapons of mass destruction in the post-conflict period, we are hopeful that a number of regimes will draw the appropriate lesson from Iraq that the pursuit of weapons of mass destruction is not in their national interest."[145]

This is an odd lesson to learn from a war in which Iraq was quite obviously attacked because it couldn't defend itself, and the attack occurred while it was disarming, in particular while it was destroying its al-Samoud 2 missiles. The lesson that those countries, and virtually every other one in the Third World, obviously learned from the war was the opposite, articulated straightforwardly by North Korea: "The Iraqi war shows that to allow disarming through inspection does not help avert a war but rather sparks it. This suggests that even the signing of a nonaggression treaty with the U.S. would not help avert a war."[146]

NORTH KOREA AND THE END OF INTERNATIONAL DISARMAMENT

North Korea, another totalitarian state that is in some ways worse than Iraq, is generally presented, even by much of the former antiwar movement, as a rogue state threatening aggression, possibly even against the United States. In fact, one staple argument against the war on Iraq was, "North Korea is a much bigger threat, so why are we attacking Iraq?"

Actually, the entire North Korean "crisis" that began in late 2002 when North Korea supposedly admitted to a U.S. official that it had nuclear weapons (North Korea denies that it did so) is a result of the Bush administration's aggressive foreign policy.

In 1994, when North Korea threatened to pull out of

the Nuclear Nonproliferation Treaty and start work on a nuclear bomb, the Clinton administration managed to make it back down in return for an agreement, known as the Agreed Framework. In return for North Korea's remaining a non-nuclear state, the United States and other countries would ship it fuel oil, the United States would provide it with two light-water nuclear reactors by 2003, and the United States would undertake not to make a nuclear first-strike on North Korea. Desperately in need of energy sources and too poor to buy oil on the world market, North Korea claimed it had little alternative to nuclear energy.

After making this agreement, the United States violated its own commitments. By 2003, there was not even a plan for obtaining the light-water reactors. More remarkable still, it had not made any assurances about a nuclear first-strike—especially surprising because the NPT, to which the United States is a signatory, explicitly requires that nuclear states not use nuclear weapons on non-nuclear states. In fact, worse than this, as covered earlier the United States had, explicitly considered the use of nuclear weapons against North Korea in the scenarios developed in the *Nuclear Posture Review*. Added to the inclusion of North Korea in the "axis of evil" in the 2002 State of the Union address and to the open desires of the neoconservatives to attack North Korea, this was enough to scare North Korea into making preparations to defend itself.

So it declared it had the right to make nuclear weapons, it announced its withdrawal from the NPT (all signatories have the right to withdraw, if they provide 90 days notice), and it closed its nuclear facilities to international inspectors.

Whether the Bush administration will feel that a war with North Korea is plausible or not remains to be seen—in addition to potential nuclear weapons, North Korea possesses a massive conventional deterrent in the form of tens of thousands of artillery pieces in range of Seoul and also in range of U.S. forces stationed on the border. The administration's decision to remove the 14,000 U.S. infantry on the border could be simply an attempt to scare the South Korean ruling elite into acquiescence to U.S. demands with regard to North Korea, but it is also seen by many as a possible prelude to war.[147]

If North Korea can avert war, it will be because it is able to defend itself; Iraq was defenseless, so it could not stop the war.

CHAPTER 7

International Law

EVER SINCE THE BUSH administration's presentation to the General Assembly on September 12, 2002, and the passage of UNSCR 1441 in November 2002, the claim that war was necessary to enforce international law and, incidentally, to make the U.N. "relevant," was high on the list of justifications.

The argument was ridiculous on its face. Iraq was threatening no country with aggression, and its only provable violations of Security Council resolutions were technical, mostly consisting of incomplete documentation about weapons that may or may not exist, and for the use of which there were no clearly manifested plans.

At the same time, other nations possess WMD and are in violation of U.N. resolutions. Israel, for example, is in ✓ violation of, at a very conservative count, over 30 resolutions, pertaining among other things to the very substantive issue of the continuing illegal occupation of another people, along with violations of the Fourth Geneva

Convention through steady encroachment on and effective annexation of that land.[148] Israel's repeated invasions and bombing of Lebanon were clear violations of U.N. resolutions in some cases and international law in every case. Indonesia, another U.S. ally, violated U.N. resolutions for a quarter of a century in East Timor with relative impunity. Morocco is illegally occupying Western Sahara. And so on. In each of these cases, the United States wouldn't be required to go to war to help uphold international law; it could start simply by terminating aid and military sales to these countries.

The United States itself is also a very odd country to claim a mandate to uphold international law. Ever since a 1986 International Court of Justice (ICJ) ruling against the United States and in favor of Nicaragua, the United States has refused to acknowledge the ICJ's authority (the $17 billion in damages it was ordered to pay were never delivered). Shortly after that judgment, the United States actually vetoed a Security Council resolution calling on states to respect international law.

Of course, the United States doesn't need to violate Security Council resolutions, since it can always veto them—as it did when the Security Council tried to condemn its blatantly illegal invasion of Panama in 1989, and on seven occasions during its contra war on Nicaragua. And throughout the recent drive to war on Iraq, the constant refrain was that the Bush administration reserved the right to go to war by itself if the

Security Council didn't decide to—even though this would place the U.S. in violation of the U.N. Charter.

Even if we take this argument seriously, however, it has severe flaws in it. For one thing, it's possible to argue that repeated U.S. violations of international law when it comes to Iraq, and in particular of the specific "containment" regime instituted after the Gulf War, released Iraq from any obligations.

To start with, Iraq was under illegal attack for the past decade with numerous bombings including the Desert Fox campaign, even while it was being called on to obey international law.

The United States also took numerous illegal and/or questionably legal steps to subvert the legal regime of "containment:" (1) passing the "Iraq Liberation Act" in October 1998, which provided $97 million for groups trying to overthrow the Iraqi government, a clear violation of Iraqi sovereignty and international law; (2) stating that only with regime change would the sanctions be lifted, in violation of UNSCR 687; and (3) using weapons inspections to commit espionage, the information from which was then used in selection of targets during Desert Fox.

Perhaps the most cogent counter to the international law argument, however, is the fact that the war was an act of premeditated aggression.

All the signs point in the same direction.

First, in August 2002, Defense Secretary Rumsfeld ordered that the list of bombing targets be extended far beyond the goal of enforcing the no-fly zones to include command-and-control centers, and in general to go beyond mere reaction to threats. According to John Pike of Globalsecurity.org, this was "part of their strategy of going ahead and softening up the air defenses now" to prepare for war later.[149] By December 2002, the shift could be noted in a 300 percent increase in tonnage of bombs dropped per threat detected—a clear sign that simply defending the overflights was no longer the primary aim of the bombings. According to the London *Guardian*, "Whitehall officials have admitted privately that the 'no-fly' patrols, conducted by RAF and U.S. aircraft from bases in Kuwait, are designed to weaken Iraq's air defence systems and have nothing to do with their stated original purpose."[150] Weakening air defense and command-and-control are the standard first steps in all U.S. wars since 1991, so the first salvoes in the war were being fired even as inspections continued. In the first two months of 2003, bombings occurred almost every other day.[151]

Next, in the wrangling at the Security Council over what was to be UNSCR 1441, the U.S. administration tried a transparent gambit that has gotten quite a workout recently. Before the war on Yugoslavia, the Clinton administration presented the Serbian government with a draft agreement (known as the Rambouillet draft after the town in which they met) that was essentially an ultimatum requiring that Serbia submit to an indefinite military occupation by NATO (read American) forces or face war.[152] Similar tactics were also tried against Afghanistan.[153]

In original drafts of UNSCR 1441, the United States included, for example, a provision that "UNMOVIC and IAEA shall have the right to declare for the purposes of freezing a site to be inspected no-fly/no-drive zones, exclusion zones, and/or ground and air transit corridors," adding that these could be enforced by "armed forces," potentially including the armed forces of an individual nation. This was correctly seen by the rest of the Security Council as a blueprint for a U.S. occupation of Iraq and was rejected, largely because of the historical experience of the Rambouillet draft.

Some have claimed that UNSCR 1441 itself was sufficient authorization for the war. This is clearly untrue; not only is there no specific language about the consequences of noncompliance, paragraphs 4, 11, 12, and 14 explicitly require that consideration of Iraqi compliance and the consequences thereof be submitted to the Security Council, not acted on by any member state.

Furthermore, the United States never intended to allow the inspection process required by 1441 to get very far. According to strategic analyst Michael Klare, all of the administration's supposed diplomatic activities regarding Iraq in the fall of 2002 and early 2003 were merely a smokescreen.[154] The war had been seriously planned from at least the spring of 2002, but in the summer there was intense serious internal debate in the military between a so-called "Afghan option," with 50–75,000 troops and heavy reliance on air power and Iraqi opposition forces, and the eventual plan, "Desert Storm lite," with 200,000–250,000 troops and a full-scale invasion.[155]

The decision was made in late August, but this more-involved plan, according to Klare, required at least a six-month deployment.[156] Ever since then, the timetable was not one of diplomacy, U.N. resolutions, and weapons inspections, but rather one of deployment, strong-arming of regional allies (especially Kuwait and Turkey) needed as staging areas for the invasion, and, quite likely, replenishment of stocks of precision weapons depleted in the war on Afghanistan (roughly 800 cruise missiles and 23,000 guided weapons were used during the war).[157]

That is why, since near the beginning of February, the constant refrain from the White House was that time was running out, that things had to be decided in a matter of "weeks, not months." This had nothing to do with any imminent threat from Iraq, nor was it a response to failure of the inspections (in fact, their effectiveness was increasing every day). It was simply because the troops were there and ready to go.

The obvious conclusion is that the war was decided on, irrespective of Iraq's actions. Nothing Iraq could have done short of full-scale capitulation and "regime change" would have stopped the United States from going to war. That makes this war a clear case of aggression.

Aggression is itself the most fundamental violation of international law. In the language of the Nuremberg Trials, it is a crime against peace. Former Supreme Court Justice Robert Jackson, chief U.S. prosecutor at the first Nuremberg trial, called waging aggressive war "the supreme international crime differing only from other war crimes in that it contains within itself the accumulated evil of the whole."

It surely is unprecedented in world history that a country has been required to disarm itself and even been castigated by the "international community" for significant though partial compliance with disarmament requirements, when all along it was under escalating attack from another nation and told repeatedly that it would be subjected to a full-scale war of aggression—and that all of this was done in the name of upholding international law.

CHAPTER 8

Democracy and Human Rights
Liberating Iraq

ANOTHER ARGUMENT FOR war soft-pedaled by the Bush administration until early March, but heavily promoted thereafter as the WMD charges fell through, was the claim that the war was to liberate Iraq. War on Iraq was needed to bring democracy and human rights to Iraq, the argument went, in order to end the suffering under the sanctions—even further, it was necessary as the first step in democratizing the Middle East and bathing it in a warm American glow.

Whether or not the administration believes its own propaganda, it plays well with a certain domestic constituency. The continued fascination of political liberals with humanitarian justifications for U.S. wars is always puzzling. Most of them know that the Vietnam War was not a humanitarian war or one fought to bring freedom and democracy to the Vietnamese. Most of them don't think that the political elites in the United States are any less rapacious now than they were then; certainly they don't think that George W. Bush is more of a humanitarian than Lyndon Johnson.

And, in fact, this is the same U.S. government whose current plans for Africa include massive pressure through the World Bank for water privatization—in an early example in Cochabamba, Bolivia, Bechtel Corp. (which is now getting major rebuilding contracts in Iraq) used its monopoly control of water to triple prices in one swoop.[158] This is the government that has, through the IMF and World Bank, steadily imposed user fees for primary education throughout Africa (thus denying the poor the right to literacy). This is the same government that fought a multi-year crusade to keep African nations from making AIDS drugs available to their populations at affordable prices (and is currently trying to restrict and limit the Doha declaration, one of the few good developments in the post-9/11 world, in which all countries agreed that every country has the right to deal with medical emergencies without regard to patent protections).[159] To think that this government is somehow motivated by concern for human rights specifically and only when it comes to going to war against other countries requires a remarkable effort of doublethink.

One might ask also, if there is such great concern for human rights, why this so rarely manifests when the United States can do something that doesn't involve war. This concern did not lead the United States to fund the Global AIDS Fund at anywhere near acceptable levels, or to cancel its part of the Third World's external debt, which is being serviced by denying the basic rights of subsistence of large numbers of people; this concern doesn't even lead the United States to terminate military and diplomatic support for countries like Israel, Egypt, Colombia, Turkey, and Saudi Arabia which commit massive human rights violations in part with equipment they get from the United States.

In my book *The New Crusade*, I studied this question, focusing on the examples of Somalia, Rwanda (where the United States actively combated attempts at preventing the genocide), Kosovo, and Afghanistan, and distilled the following principles of U.S. humanitarian intervention:

> ➤ The humanitarian crisis is an excuse, not a reason. The United States intervenes when it sees something to gain, frequently economic and political control or a military foothold.

> ➤ The United States doesn't particularly care whether its intervention ameliorates the humanitarian crisis or exacerbates it. The intervention is structured primarily to serve the aforementioned interest.

> ➤ The United States has little interest in traditional humanitarian and peacekeeping methods, which involve a patient presence on the ground. Such interventions don't serve the purpose of gaining greater power and control. A massive use

of military force, on the other hand, always benefits the United States as an empire by showing its willingness to use force, its devastating superiority, and most of all, its impunity.[160]

There are two separate questions we have to consider in looking at the "liberation" of Iraq. First, the idea that U.S. intervention was to create democracy. Second, the idea that it was to help the Iraqi people—after all, one could always argue that even if the United States exerts total control over Iraq, it might be better for the people than was living under Saddam Hussein. Conversely, one could argue that the United States is passionately committed to fostering democracy but doesn't care about basic economic or social rights.

DEMOCRACY

Historically, the United States has had a relatively clear policy toward democracy in Iraq and the Middle East— hostility and subversion. In 1953, the CIA sponsored a coup in Iran that overthrew a democratically elected prime minister and instituted a monarchist police state. In 1958, when a massive Iraqi popular uprising overthrew the Hashemite monarchy, which was essentially subservient to Britain, the United States reacted by sending 14,000 Marines to Lebanon as a show of force and initiating proceedings for a coup against the populist military leader who came to power, Abdel Karim Qassem. In 1963, in a coup by the Ba'ath Party with CIA assistance, Qassem was deposed and murdered (Ali Saleh Sa'adi, then secretary general of the Iraqi Ba'ath Party, said "We came to power on a CIA train").[161]

After the Gulf War, George Bush Sr., made a call to the Iraqi military and people (the original plan was to appeal just to the military) to rise up and overthrow the Iraqi government. Iraqis did exactly that, in what later came to be known as the Iraqi intifada. Starting with disaffected soldiers returning from the Gulf War, it quickly spread to engulf the south, where the Shia majority of Iraq is most concentrated. Within weeks, the revolt included Kurds in the north and even a small number of Sunni Arabs. It was the most serious threat Hussein's rule had faced.

It's widely admitted that the United States stood by and allowed the rebels to be massacred by loyal remnants of the Iraqi army (mostly the Republican Guard). In fact, U.S. complicity in the maintenance of Hussein in power goes far deeper than that. After the war, with allied forces occupying southern Iraq, a no-fly order had been imposed, but in early March 1991 General Norman Schwarzkopf partially rescinded that order, limiting it to fixed-wing aircraft, a move that allowed the Iraqi government to use helicopter gunships to mow down the rebels.

The U.S. military took a number of other steps that helped Hussein to beat down the uprising. According to a former Iraqi army major who defected and joined the rebels, the Americans were not neutral: "Their behavior amounted to malevolent interference without the use of arms... In Nassiriyah, U.S. aircraft flew over Iraqi helicopters and gave them protection. American troops stopped the rebels from reaching an arms depot to obtain ammunition. The American and French troops still in southern Iraq dug trenches to slow down the rebels and stop them from pursuing Saddam's troops. Finally, American troops provided Saddam's Republican Guard with safe passage through their lines to attack rebel positions."[162]

Not only were the rebels prevented from raiding arms depots, on occasion they were forcibly disarmed by allied forces.[163] There can be little doubt that, far from making a series of unaccountable mistakes, the United States moved deliberately to keep Hussein in power, and thus shares responsibility for the massacres committed by Iraqi government forces.

In 1996, Brent Scowcroft, national security adviser at the time of the intifada, told ABC Television, "I frankly wished [the uprising] hadn't happened. I envisioned a postwar government being a military government."[164] Months later, Thomas Friedman of the *New York Times* encapsulated official reasoning with his characteristic flair: Washington, he said, wanted "the best of all worlds: an iron-fisted Iraqi junta without Saddam Hussein."[165] A government headed by Hussein, while not as good as a pro-American military government without Hussein, was far better for the administration than a government created by a popular uprising, which might have defended the rights of its people.

This record dovetails with a well-documented enmity to democracy in other parts of the world—as epitomized by, *inter alia*, U.S.-backed coups in 1954 in Guatemala, 1960 in Laos, 1964 in Brazil, 1973 in Chile. Of course, one might decide that, though previous administrations had little concern for democracy, this new administration is different—and it's certainly true that the neoconservatives uniformly condemn the previous stabilization of Saddam Hussein's regime. Thus, it's important to look at the record since 9/11, and, in particular, to understand the true meaning of "regime change."

We should start by recognizing that the United States does not have any particular ideological opposition to democracy. In general, it simply fosters the government that will allow it the most political control and the most benefits for U.S. corporations—subject sometimes to concerns about stability of the regime, if it is too oppressive. These considerations led the United States to install in Japan and Germany more democratic regimes than existed in 1945.

They were not, however, real democracies, and especially in Japan, were not responsive to the will of the people. Chalmers Johnson's excellent book, *Blowback*, describes the manner in which the wishes of the Japanese people were set aside when the United States wished to obtain passage of the 1960 Mutual Cooperation and

Security Treaty that permanently cemented Japan's role in the structure of U.S. military/political influence in East Asia. Japan's political system still bears the stigmata of a U.S.-imposed "democracy" from above, as Junichiro Koizumi, the Prime Minister, showed when he defied the wishes of over 80 percent of the population to support the war on Iraq.

Iraq is like Japan and Germany in that the system instituted could hardly be less democratic than the one that preceded it, and also in that the system will be imposed from above. As we covered in the introduction, it will, if anything, be even more directly subservient to U.S. dictates.

UNDERSTANDING "REGIME CHANGE"

Even in the twenty-first century, the method of control is not always more subtle than in the past—we have already covered the administration's involvement in the coup attempt in Venezuela. In Palestine, as we mentioned before, attempts are underway to recreate the neocolonial-style client government that existed throughout the duration of the Oslo process until it broke down in 2000.

The sham of democracy engineered in Afghanistan was, in a way, almost cruder than the coup attempt. The *loya jirga*, or grand council, that selected the current interim government of Afghanistan, was peopled from the start with delegates selected by the United States, mostly representatives of the regional warlords, with a sprinkling of Afghan expatriates (mostly from the United States) and "technocrats" to give it some aura of respectability. Representatives from the 1.5-million-strong Watan Party, successor to the People's Democratic Party of Afghanistan (the Communist party that ruled Afghanistan until 1992), were not allowed as delegates.

According to Omar Zakhilwal and Adeena Niazi, delegates to the *loya jirga*, "We delegates were denied anything more than a symbolic role in the selection process. A small group of Northern Alliance chieftains decided everything behind closed doors." Since former monarch Zahir Shah, the most popular candidate for interim president, was unsuitable to U.S. interests, "the entire *loya jirga* was postponed for almost two days while the former king was strong-armed into renouncing any meaningful role in the government."[166]

When U.S. special envoy to Afghanistan Zalmay Khalilzad (later special envoy to the Iraqi opposition) suddenly announced to the world media that Zahir Shah was stepping down—something that the octogenarian former king was apparently unable to say for himself—there was no doubt who was running the show. Hamid Karzai, the handpicked candidate of the United States, was swiftly confirmed. And any lingering doubt about Karzai's freedom of action should have been ended by the news that U.S. Special Forces were acting as his bodyguards. Later, those Special Forces were replaced with private mercenaries hired by Dyncorp, an American military contractor.[167]

In the current dominant mode of global control, power is exercised mainly through economic means, mostly through multilateral institutions like the IMF, World Bank, and World Trade Organization. As a result of IMF/World Bank structural adjustment in the 1980s and '90s and even more because of the proliferation of "free trade" agreements in the '90s—the process usually referred to as globalization—the world had come to the point where, before 9/11, the U.S. Treasury Department had more control over the economic decisions of Third World countries than did the duly elected governments of those countries—with the partial exception of the Middle East and Central Asia, where "globalization" had made much less of a dent. With their freedom of action taken away, it didn't matter who was elected to rule in most Third World countries; no longer could they try seriously to implement a substantial reform program dedicated to improving human welfare.

This mode of control doesn't much appeal to the Bush administration or to the neoconservatives because it frequently involves multilateral institutions that are at least nominally not under total U.S. control (although the IMF comes close) and because it has been ineffective in penetrating the societies where most of the world's oil lies— and possibly even in part because those multilateral institutions have become the target of socially conscious global justice activists. This administration prefers, as in the days of the Cold War in East Asia, the creation of governments that fit very closely, and are very tightly constrained, within a military framework of U.S. global hegemony. And that is what is unfolding in Afghanistan, Iraq and quite possibly the rest of the Middle East.

HUMAN RIGHTS AND HUMANITARIAN CONCERNS

Even on the question of civil and political rights (as opposed to the economic and social rights that have equal status in terms of international law), the Bush administration's newfound concern for Iraqi liberation lacks credibility. So militant, in fact, was its indifference that when, in October 2002, Hussein took the unthinkable step of issuing a general pardon to Iraqi prisoners, there was no reaction from the administration. So fervent was the response of the Iraqi public to the prisoner releases that authorities at Abu Ghraib prison outside of Baghdad lost control of the process as the crowd grabbed iron bars and started breaking down the prison walls.[168] The move was in part clearly a trial balloon; when Hussein saw that the release made not the slightest difference to the administration he stopped further releases and, according to some reports, started having some prisoners quietly rearrested.[169] In this case, some verbal acknowledgment by the Bush government might have been the only "intervention" needed to protect human rights.

The larger humanitarian justifications for the war can be illuminated perfectly by considering a specific incident during the war. U.S.-British bombing had knocked out power in Basra, leading to the collapse of water treatment and pumping (a situation that persisted for weeks).[170] Because of the putative need for the British to fix this situation, the British area commander declared Basra a "military target."[171]

Andrew Natsios, head administrator of the U.S. Agency for International Development (USAID), held a press conference in which he touched on the problems of Basra, where only 40 percent of the population had access to potable water. The genesis of these problems, according to him, was "a deliberate decision by the regime not to repair the water system or replace old equipment with new equipment, so in many cases people are basically drinking untreated sewer water in their homes and have been for some years."[172]

This took the mendacity of the regime to new heights. As we saw in detail in an earlier, ever since Iraq's water treatment system was left in shambles by Gulf War I, where the deliberate targeting of the entire electrical power grid caused water pumping to shut down and sewage to fill the streets of Basra, the Iraqi government had scrambled desperately to repair its water system, but was systematically blocked in such attempts by the United States.

The similarities to the larger picture should be clear. To say that the deaths of 500,000 children due to the sanctions were a price worth paying, as then U.S. Ambassador to the U.N. Madeleine Albright did, and then to claim that the United States went to war to liberate the Iraqis is the most obscene hypocrisy.

The sanctions were imposed as a deliberate instrument of U.S. control in the region and kept on for 12 years largely by the political will of the United States. Their consequences were not only foreseeable but explicitly predicted. At every stage of the way, the United States manipulated the process to make Iraq bite harder. First, it refused to allow sufficient oil sales to make the Oil for Food program acceptable to Iraq. Then, it used its power to impose "holds" to keep Iraqi society from reconstructing and even went so far as to keep out medicine and vaccines—up through the end of 2002, when it put up impediments to the import of basic antibiotics like streptomycin.

The claim that the war was "humane" or "humanitarian" rests fundamentally on a certain dehistoricization—that the war must be detached from the context of U.S. policy that led to it, and in particular from the brutally destructive sanctions. This "change of course" doctrine is an argument from historical amnesia; it requires that one refuse to perceive that the structure of U.S. society and the elite interests that drive foreign policy have not changed in any fundamental sense. In this case, it is, of course, far more logical to see the war as a culmination of the sanctions, replacing partial U.S. control with near complete U.S. control.

It is also true that the conduct of the war was not humane either. The relentless shelling of Baghdad, the use of cluster bombs in residential areas,[173] and the hysterical attacks on civilian vehicles after the first suicide attack at a U.S. military checkpoint were all clear violations of humanitarian principles.[174] The Iraq Body Count Project (www.iraqbodycount.net), working only from corroborated media reports, estimates (as of May 1, 2003) the number of civilians killed in the war to be between 2,180 and 2,653. This does not include unreported deaths, indirect deaths due to loss of electricity and water, or the massive number of deaths of the Iraqi military, which should certainly be counted in an unnecessary war against a foe that had made no aggressive moves.

The deaths caused by the war itself, however, is nothing compared with those caused by previous policies. The basic political principle that underlies U.S. policy is "casualty management"; the United States must be careful in making its targeting decisions when waging a war, because of the potential backlash, but it needs to exercise much less care when it kills people through lack of access to medicine, water, or food. As long as the American public cannot see all of the deaths and suffering caused as the results of a unified policy, and instead tries to impute the lion's share of it to some nebulous other source, humanitarian intervention will live on as a justification for future wars.

Given the reality of states around the world that brutally oppress their populaces, an alternative is needed. Unfortunately, as I discuss in *The New Crusade*, the United States systematically undermines any attempts to create a more equitable international basis for humanitarian intervention. It is unbelievable effrontery to create the conditions for disaster through exploitation and constant maneuvering for political gain, simultaneously sabotaging any effective, democratic international mechanism for dealing with human rights problems that arise, and then to carry out profoundly destructive "humanitarian" interventions. To have any credibility at all, the United States must start showing humanitarian intent in situations it does not benefit from or try to control.

There is a place, at least in theory, for the international community to intervene to protect human rights. There is a place for peacekeeping and for humanitarian intervention. There is no place for exercises in U.S. or Western domination, whether economic or military, under the guise of protecting human rights.

The basic error in accepting humanitarian justifications for U.S. intervention is the lingering unstated assumption, shared by so many, that the U.S. government has good intentions for the rest of the world.

CHAPTER 9

Oil as a Component of Empire

AFTER DISPOSING OF the various justifications given for the war, we are faced with the obvious question: What was it really about?

We have already outlined the principles of the new imperial vision—overwhelming military superiority, frequent "regime change," an expanding ring of military bases, and, very clearly, maximal control over world oil production and transport. The war on Iraq served all of the latter three purposes.

Such is the state of mainstream political discourse that any intimation that oil might have something to do with the war is immediately branded a "conspiracy theory." This is rather inexplicable, given that even the most orthodox defenders of the status quo freely admit that economic interests shape policy. Foreign aid is often cited as an example of America's disinterested generosity (though the United States contributes a lower fraction of its GNP than any other First World country), but even USAID states openly that the principal beneficiary of its operations are American corporations. For some reason, though, this conventional wisdom is conveniently forgotten on the frequent occasions when the United States goes to war.

OIL AND HISTORICAL U.S. MIDDLE EAST POLICY

Actually, it has never been a secret that U.S. Middle East policy revolves around oil. Strong U.S. interest in the region's oil dates from after World War I, in particular after the 1920 San Remo agreement, in which Britain and France essentially divided the oil of the Middle East between them. Britain had early on established the standard colonial means of dealing with oil; pressuring a weak, corrupt government to grant an oil concession, essentially a deal whereby some corporation gained the right to all the oil that lay under the land in the area covered by the concession, and was required to pay only token royalties to the government of the country. In the first 50 years of Middle East oil concessions, Western corporations and a small ruling elite in the Middle East got very rich, but the people benefited minimally if at all.

Unhappy U.S. oil companies complained strenuously about their exclusion, and through the intervention of the U.S. government (Herbert Hoover played a major role in this), replaced the San Remo agreement with the 1928 "Red-line" agreement, which gave them a 23.5 percent share of all oil concessions in the former Ottoman Empire (excluding Kuwait); later this agreement came to apply only to Iraq. In 1933, Texaco and Chevron gained the ultimate prize—a 60-year concession on the lion's share of Saudi oil, which they later shared with Exxon and Mobil in the formation of Aramco.[175] Around that time, Gulf also obtained 50 percent of the Kuwaiti concession.

World War II brought the strategic significance of oil into sharp relief, as availability of supplies was often the determining factor in military engagements. Though the United States produced almost two-thirds of the world's oil at the time, it moved very firmly to maintain and extend control over Middle East oil, already seen as the largest supply in the world. In 1943, in an attempt to woo Ibn Saud, President Franklin Roosevelt made Saudi Arabia eligible for Lend-Lease aid by declaring its defense to be of vital interest to the United States; in 1945, after the Yalta Conference, he personally visited Ibn Saud.

The significance of Saudi oil was already clear—a 1945 State Department document called it "a stupendous source of strategic power, and one of the greatest material prizes in world history."[176]

In 1951, Iran nationalized its oil, whose concession had belonged to British Petroleum. Oil companies colluded to embargo Iran's oil, and the country suffered without oil income for two years until a joint U.S.-British coup toppled the democratically elected government and restored the tyrannical Shah Reza Pahlavi to power. The post-coup division gave rights over 40 percent of Iran's oil to American companies.

The 1958 uprising in Iraq, mentioned earlier, directly imperiled the Anglo-American condominium over the region's oil, whence the strenuous reaction from the United States. Qassem, Iraq's ruler at the time, antagonized the oil companies further in 1961 with the passage of Law 80, which nationalized the oil lying under the 99.5 percent of Iraq's land that was then largely unexplored and not in production. As mentioned before, he paid for his temerity.

By the 1970s, the strategic situation and U.S. power in the Middle East had changed dramatically. The United States was bogged down in Vietnam, Britain had withdrawn its troops from the region (although Israel had emerged as a new military power at the same time), and the Soviet Union was playing a newly assertive role. In 1971, Libya nationalized a British Petroleum concession; in 1972, Iraq completed its nationalization; in 1975, Kuwait and Venezuela nationalized; and by 1980, Saudi Arabia had as well. The United States was able to make only symbolic gestures in response, like placing Iraq on the State Department's list of state sponsors of terrorism.

In 1980, responding to the Soviet invasion of Afghanistan, the Carter Doctrine was promulgated: "An attempt by an outside force to gain control of the Persian Gulf region will be regarded as an assault on the vital interests of the United States of America." This was followed by implementation of plans to create a Rapid Deployment Force, which eventually evolved into the Central Command, the organization in charge of prosecuting Gulf Wars 1 and 2.

Gulf War 1 obtained for the U.S. military a permanent land-based presence in the Middle East, gave the United States partial control over Iraqi oil (through the U.N. sanctions), and enhanced the power of Saudi Arabia, a longtime U.S. ally, in the global oil market.

SOME COMMON MISCONCEPTIONS

Although oil is the primary consideration in U.S. Middle East policy, it is very far from true that oil companies determine that policy. Kissinger's pronounced tilt toward Israel in the early 1970s was strenuously opposed by the oil companies, which feared exactly the wave of nationalizations that occurred. In 1996, Congress passed the Iran-Libya Sanctions Act, signed by Bill Clinton, which levied a host of potential economic sanctions on any company investing more than $40 million in development of these countries' petroleum resources. In practice, the act has helped keep U.S. oil companies out of exploration deals in Iran, while not stopping European oil companies, and companies like Dick Cheney's Halliburton have lobbied against it for years without success. And, of course, the sanctions on Iraq had the effect of tilting the playing field against U.S. oil companies seeking Iraqi oil concessions.

It's also not true that the United States always pursues a "cheap oil" policy—in fact, since the United States has always been a major oil producer, there are conflicting imperatives. From 1959 to 1973, the United States had mandatory oil import controls, which made the price of oil in the United States generally more than double what it was on the world market.[177] In 1986, Saudi Arabia caused the oil price to collapse through its move to "netback pricing" and domestic U.S. oil producers were hit very hard. The same year, then Vice President George Bush personally visited Saudi Arabia, probably to threaten the Saudis with imposition of an oil tariff if they didn't do something to raise prices.[178] U.S. policy on pricing is not far from the stated policy of OPEC—the price of oil should stay in a relatively stable band, not too high or too low.

Furthermore, U.S. Middle East policy is also not about access to oil. For a time, hardly a week went by when some conservative columnist didn't discover anew that oil is bought and sold in a world market and that therefore the source of the oil is largely unimportant—and even that the United States was a major buyer of Iraqi oil.

Even as it extends its control over Middle East oil, however, the United States has always deliberately followed a policy of getting oil from sources as close to home as possible. First, it supported the domestic oil industry with the abovementioned measures, then it developed Venezuela (the chief oil exporter before 1970) as its primary source of imports.

More recently, cultivation of West African oil producers (natural sources for the United States because their proximity to it means that transport costs are low) is another significant part of Bush administration strategy. Originally, the administration had publicly written Africa off as devoid of strategic interest for the United States, but when Colin Powell went to address the World Summit on Sustainable Development, it was no accident that the two countries he visited were Gabon and Angola, both oil producers. The United States is the primary source of foreign direct investment in Angola and its chief customer. Nigeria is another major source of U.S. imports. Even after the war on Iraq started, Bush met with the president of Cameroon to discuss a major new pipeline from Chad through Cameroon to the Atlantic coast—the lion's share of the hundreds of thousands of barrels a day produced will undoubtedly be bought by the United States.[179]

OIL AND THE WAR

So in what exact way is oil the basis of U.S. Middle East policy and the war on Iraq?

To start, Iraq's posted proven reserves of 112.5 billion barrels are the second largest in the world, but according to the U.S. Energy Information Administration (USEIA), its "probable" and "possible" reserves may total 220 billion barrels (there is much controversy over these figures because of the notoriously nontransparent accounting methods of most OPEC countries). Its history has made it a largely untapped source. In the 1960s, partly because of the aforementioned Law 80, Western oil companies refused to develop much of Iraq's oil or to "lift" significant amounts from the country. In the 1980s, during the brutal war with Iran, significant exploration was not possible, and pumping capacity declined. In the 1990s, sanctions made exploration impossible once again. As a result, only 15 of the 73 oilfields discovered in Iraq have been developed. Roughly 2,000 wells have been drilled in Iraq, compared to 1 million in Texas.[180]

Thus, all oil-based considerations are magnified by the scope of the prize involved. There are at least four such considerations to which the war was relevant:

> Oil as a material prize: The war will give U.S. oil companies a role in exploiting Iraq's oil.
> Oil as a political lever: U.S. occupation of Iraq, followed by installation of a puppet regime, will give it tremendous influence over the flow of Iraq's oil. Accompanied by other moves (below), it may enable the United States to replace OPEC as the controlling force in the global oil market. In a loose sense, one can say that the war makes Iraq part of NATO (whether or not if formally joins; the relevant feature is domination by the U.S. military) and the United States part of OPEC.

➤ Oil and the euro: Denomination of oil in dollars helps to support a strong dollar even while the United States runs massive current account deficits. A switch to denomination in euros is less likely if the United States extends its control over world oil.

➤ Oil and growing world demand: U.S. policies in the Middle East, combined with indigenous factors, have combined to keep pumping capacity in the Middle East low, at just the time when world demand for Middle East oil is projected to grow by leaps and bounds. This could easily be addressed by investment, especially if the Gulf states repatriated just a fraction of their massive stores of flight capital, but war followed by investment will give the United States a much greater stake in the process.

OIL AS A MATERIAL PRIZE

There are two components to the question of oil as a material prize: First, the profits to be made on oil concessions (oil is unique among commodities in that the primary source of profits is the "downstream" production, not the "upstream" refining and retail marketing); and second, the investment of petrodollars. Both considerations militate for the long-term U.S. strategy of propping up despotic but weak feudal elites throughout the region. At first, these feudal elites, uninterested in the well-being of their populations, signed sweetheart deals with Western oil companies. Later, as the elites began to appropriate a larger share of the profits and especially after the nationalizations of the 1970s, the consideration was that these elites would happily invest those profits in the United States and Europe rather than in regional development.

In the 1990s, Saudi Arabia and the small Gulf states recycled tens of billions of petrodollars into the United States in arms transactions alone. Currently, it is estimated that total Arab flight capital is somewhere from $1–1.2 trillion,[181] a staggering figure and at least twice the GDP of the Arab world. Unlike the oil concessions, which benefit specifically oil companies, these petrodollar investments benefit all First World corporations.

Arms sales and petrodollar investments help to explain one of the natural questions from those who disbelieve that U.S. Middle East policy is about hardheaded measures to enjoy the benefits of the region's oil: If U.S. Middle East policy is about oil, why didn't the United States use the leverage it had over Kuwait after the Iraqi invasion to force Kuwait to denationalize? Not only would such an overtly colonial move have caused tremendous political difficulties, it would have gained little for corporate America, because Kuwait already invests its oil wealth there.

Since numerous companies with nationalized oil began looking into oil exploration deals with major foreign corporations during the 1990s, the issue of direct profits has regained greater importance. In that regard, the United States has put itself in a curious bind; the sanctions on Iraq and Iran shut U.S. oil companies out of the exploration deals both countries were offering, and for a time there seemed to be no political way out. That's why Vice President Cheney complained about sanctions, especially unilateral sanctions, when he was the head of Halliburton, saying that they penalized U.S. companies.[182]

"Regime change" in Iraq may be the magic bullet with regard to both Iraq and Iran. There's little doubt that the U.S. military occupation will give significant leverage to U.S. corporations in access to oil concessions. As of October 2002, Iraq had signed a total of $38 billion worth of oil deals on new fields with a potential production capacity of 4.7 million barrels per day (mbd), compared with a current theoretical maximum capacity of 2.8–2.9 mbd.[183] None of them are with American companies. The biggest are with the Russian company Lukoil, on the West Qurna oilfield, which has an estimated 11–15 billion barrels (this was recently cancelled by Iraq, but other Russian companies are vying for it) and the French TotalFinaElf, on the Majnoon field, with an estimated 12–30 billion barrels.

Despite an attempt in much of the press to give the impression that the only role of oil in the "negotiations" over Iraq was the greedy desire of France and Russia to keep their concessions, even before the war there was much talk about a role for U.S. oil companies[184]—Ahmed Chalabi, long looking forward to his self-conceived future role as Iraq's leader, told *The Washington Post* as early as September 2002 that "American companies will have a big shot at Iraqi oil."[185] In October 2002, British Petroleum's chief executive, concerned about such reports, publicly warned the United States that "there should be a level playing field for the selection of oil companies"[186] for postwar Iraqi oil concessions.

In this regard, it's worth noting that one significant effect of the sanctions on Iraq, other than giving Saudi Arabia extra money to spend in the United States, was to partly break Iraqi control of its own oil during the 1990s and the early twenty-first century. Though the oil technically remained nationalized, Iraq needed the permission of the U.N. Sanctions Committee to sell its oil, and the proceeds went to a bank account administered by the committee—which essentially means administered by the United States. No decisions about investment in equipment or exploration could realistically be made against the will of the United States. Regime change will further the project of minimizing indigenous control over the oil of Iraq.

A U.S. war on Iraq would almost complete a military encirclement of Iran (the United States will have troops in Turkey, Iraq, Afghanistan, Pakistan, and even a few in Turkmenistan, as well as on the Persian Gulf and the Strait of Hormuz, through which most Iranian oil tankers pass). Neoconservatives are already looking to the possibility of using that leverage to push Iran into the U.S. sphere.

The profits to be made by U.S. oil companies are, in themselves, an insufficient reason for the war. Obviously, many of those companies would do better, at least in the short term, if the cost of the war and the occupation likely to come after were just given to them. Though it is often necessary that the state act as an inefficient and indirect source of corporate subsidy, because a direct giveaway would cause political problems, there are also much more significant considerations.

OIL AS A POLITICAL LEVER

Going back to the State Department quote, one should note that it focuses on the oil as a "stupendous source of strategic power," with the "material prize" part as an afterthought. Oil is not only the most traded commodity in terms of value in the world, it is by far the most important strategic commodity, because every country requires oil to run. Control the flow of oil to a country and you have a knife to its jugular; controlling the price of oil also gives significant political leverage.

Since the most powerful entities that depend on Middle East oil are the European Union, Japan, and more recently China, control of Middle East oil is presumably primarily directed at them as competitors or potential competitors.

Simple military presence in the region is one very important mechanism of control. Since Gulf War 1, with the U.S. military right there, Saudi Arabia has made all of its decisions about production quotas (and thus about prices, since Saudi Arabia is the 800-pound gorilla of the world oil market) in accord with U.S. expectations. For a while, every time Iraq announced a production cut on political grounds, which would have increased the price of oil, Saudi Arabia would increase production. In late February 2003, it promised U.S. officials that in the event of war with Iraq it would boost production by 1.5 million barrels a day (mbd), largely making up for the Iraqi production at the time of 2.2 mbd.[187] Earlier, there had been times, as in 1973 with the embargo, when Saudi Arabia did not so closely follow U.S. wishes.

Regime change in Iraq might also lead to Iraq's exit from OPEC and a dramatic increase in its daily production (OPEC members voluntarily limit their production to keep the price of oil in a price band; in general, they produce a much smaller fraction of their reserves per year than non-OPEC members). Iraq might then act as a counterbalance to OPEC, dramatically reducing the possibility of independent action by the cartel. Combined with increasing U.S.-directed production in Central Asia, Angola and Cameroon (all not in OPEC) and possibly the wooing of Nigeria[188] to leave OPEC, the war could be a mechanism to transfer a significant amount of direct power over the world oil market from OPEC to the United States (through a puppet regime and through U.S. oil companies).

OIL AND THE EURO

Another oil-related concern is a bit abstruse. Currently, world oil prices are denominated in dollars. This means that the United States has the unique privilege of being able simply to print money and get oil for it. Since the mid-1980s, the United States has run a massive current account deficit. In 2002, the trade deficit hit $435.2 billion, the largest ever—and the current account deficit was over $500 billion (current account is simply the difference between net receipts from the rest of the world and net payments to it—it differs slightly from the trade deficit because some financial flows are involved).[189]

Normal countries cannot sustain such a deficit for so long without significant devaluation of their currency, yet throughout the 1990s the dollar remained strong. There is at least some reason to believe that dollar denomination of oil has something to do with that, although the dollar's strength is undoubtedly in part an indirect effect of the overwhelming political and military power of the United States, which helps to cause massive inflows of foreign investment.

With the advent of the euro in 2000, this could potentially change. In fact, Iraq moved immediately to start denominating its oil sales in euros, as a political statement against the United States. Later, Iran and Venezuela, both with their own concerns about U.S. policy, also began to consider such a shift (oddly, North Korea denominates its imports in euros as well). Had three significant oil-producing countries started using euros, this would have put major pressure on the dollar. This consideration has been treated by some as "the" reason for the war; certainly, this is not the case. In fact, the effect of the war on this question may well be ambiguous; it is the increased belligerence of U.S. policy that made Iraq switch and Iran and Venezuela consider switching, but, on the other hand, if Iraq becomes a large producer closely linked with the United States, the leverage of the United States to oppose switching to the euro will be substantial. This question is also closely linked with and subordinate to the larger one of control of oil. To go further, dollar hegemony in general, whether through the use of the dollar as a global reserve currency, the increasing number of countries that peg their currency to the dollar, or the dollar denomination of the world oil market is simply a reflection of broader U.S. political hegemony, although it is an important prop for the U.S. economy.[190]

OIL, GROWING WORLD DEMAND, AND THE MIDDLE EAST

Although the war is not about access to oil, the final reason does relate to the amount of oil on the world market. World oil consumption is growing rapidly, but non-OPEC production has already peaked. The Middle East has two-thirds of the world's oil reserves and will be increasingly important as a source of oil in the future—according to the

Bush-Cheney energy policy, by 2020 Persian Gulf oil will supply between 54 and 67 percent of world needs. According to the USEIA, world oil consumption will increase from 75 mbd in 1999 to 119 in 2020. Thus, Middle East production will have to be dramatically higher.

And yet, for a variety of reasons, OPEC production capacity is lower in 2003 than it was in 1980.[191] Saudi Arabia is generally considered to have done well in increasing its own capacity, but it's about the only one. Iran's and Iraq's have dramatically deteriorated.

In part, this problem can be traced to U.S. policy. The Iran-Iraq war, which the United States fully supported, led to permanent decreases in the capacity of both countries. The sanctions on Iraq and Iran have made further exploration and development more difficult for Iran and impossible for Iraq. The smaller Gulf states have little reason to substantially increase their capacity, since they have only minuscule populations to provide for. The encouragement of investing petrodollars in foreign countries has left the region short of capital for further oil exploration.

With spare capacity almost nil (only Saudi Arabia has any noticeable amount), a massive increase in production capacity is necessary, unless major cuts in consumption (necessary also to halt global warming) are made.

Even in the absence of this new war, many OPEC members have been looking to welcome foreign corporations. Venezuela, beset by the same lack of indigenous capital-formation that seems to have afflicted most Third World countries in recent years, needed foreign investment in the early '90s to increase its production capacity. Iran and Iraq are seeking foreign investment. Even Saudi Arabia, which categorically refuses to consider giving exploration concessions on oil, did briefly explore natural gas concessions with ExxonMobil, Shell, and others.[192]

Although war is not necessary to increase the production capacity of the Middle East, or even of Iraq, it is necessary if the United States is to maintain control of that process.

Combining the growing foreign investment with the planned increase in U.S. control of oil, what is really on the horizon is a colonial re-appropriation of the Middle East's energy reserves. The grand ideological visions of the neoconservatives dovetail perfectly with the requirements of the powers-that-be in the global economy, the fruits of U.S. policies in the region, and the designs of Western, especially American, oil companies.

Oil is certainly behind this war, but primarily oil as a component of empire and only secondarily oil as a component of the venality of Dick Cheney, Halliburton, and the U.S. oil majors.

CONCLUSION

The New Imperialism

IT HAS ALREADY become passé to say that the Bush administration's foreign policy is a new imperialism. Mainstream politicians, like the head of the Liberal Democrats in Britain, use the term. Journalists like Jay Bookman, deputy editor of the *Atlanta Journal-Constitution*, use it.[193] Even defenders of the policy use it—like Michael Ignatieff, writing in the *New York Times* Sunday magazine about the "case for a liberal imperialism."

It is a new imperialism that smacks of colonialism in many ways. It also involves a remarkable rhetorical arrogance of an extreme unilateralist nature.

And yet, business as usual continues—it was never likely that the map of the Middle East would be redrawn, and clearly the territorial integrity of Iraq has been preserved. U.S. economic domination of the world continues. And, in fact, the major elements of the new military imperialism were prefigured in the second Clinton administration. The increase in military spending started then, as did "NATO expansion," so clearly revealed by the political machinations over the "coalition of the willing" to be an instrument, along with European Union (EU) expansion, of U.S. political influence over the EU. Similarly with international law—in fact, though the "multilateralist" Bill Clinton openly flouted the Security Council in the 1998 Desert Fox campaign and ignored it in the 1999 war on Yugoslavia, the "unilateralist" George W. Bush went to the Security Council for a resolution on Iraq.

Furthermore, U.S. policies since World War II have always been imperial, although often more subtly so than now.[194] In a 1948 policy planning document, George Kennan laid out the reasoning quite straightforwardly (in the context of the "Far East," but it generalizes easily):

> We have about 50 percent of the world's wealth but only 6.3 percent of its population.... In this situation we cannot fail to be the object of envy and resentment. Our real task in the coming period is to devise a pattern of relationships which will permit us to maintain this position of disparity without positive detriment to our national security. To do so we will have to dispense with all sentimentality and daydreaming, and our attention will have to be concentrated everywhere on our immediate national objec-

tives. We need not deceive ourselves that we can afford the luxury of altruism and world benefaction.

He went on to add, "We should cease to talk about such vague and—for the Far East—unreal objectives as human rights, the raising of living standards and democratization. The day is not far off when we are going to have to deal in straight power concepts. The less we are then hampered by idealistic slogans, the better."[195] As amply documented, most particularly by Noam Chomsky, the "pattern of relationships" involved the running of other countries' economies to serve the needs of U.S. corporations, and the establishment of this pattern has required the use of everything from subversion and manipulation to extreme force.

So, what's so special about this new brand of imperialism?

Unipolarity: This is the underlying and defining characteristic, which enables all the others. When the Soviet Union existed, there were two differences. The minor one was that the Soviet Union was at least potentially a military counterbalance. This rarely manifested, because the Soviet Union usually conducted itself as a regional power, not a world superpower. It didn't even interfere when the United States dramatically increased its influence with the 1953 coup in Iran. It interfered minimally in the Vietnam War. But there was the potential, sometimes exercised—it did put a stop to the 1973 Yom Kippur war before Egypt could be crushed. Its existence was always at least a partial deterrent to U.S. use of military force.

More important, it posed an ideological challenge. So American citizens had to live better than Soviet citizens; even more important, U.S. satellites had to be, at least in some cases like South Korea and Taiwan, better off than Soviet satellites. Now, with no force to oppose it, there need be no limit to the virulence of U.S. imperialism. Europe was rebuilt and simultaneously brought into the American sphere after World War II at significant cost, but Afghanistan will not be reconstructed even for a paltry few billion dollars, even though its significance as a breeding ground for radical Islamism is obvious. In Iraq, the oil industry will be reconstructed and, because of public pressure, some token efforts at general rehabilitation will be made, but the country will almost certainly be left in a shattered state, with an underclass increasingly unable to fend for itself. The United States need not even make the token efforts toward a welfare state that were necessary in the bipolar world.

And, of course, the United States need not be deterred from any future war simply by the threat of resistance from an equal. So a series of small wars against helpless or almost helpless targets is a real possibility—Iran, Syria, Libya, North Korea. The normal political constraints will largely be ignored, although, of course, military realities like North Korea's significant deterrent capability must still be taken into account.

Commitment to maintaining this unipolarity is another feature of the new imperialism. There are two potential threats—the European Union and China (with Japan a distant third). So far, the EU is primarily an economic threat, which we will treat below. The main endgame goal of the architects of the neoconservative foreign policy is China, the only major country that can independently resist U.S. domination. If China is "contained," then, in the neoconservative fantasies, resistance will be impossible.

Pre-emption and other imperial declarations: There is no longer any pretense that the United States acts in response to threats posed by others: "In the post-Cold War era, America and its allies...have become the primary objects of deterrence." It is the assertion of a U.S. right to aggression, not even subject to meaningful consultation with longstanding European allies. The new policy of "regime change" is similar—it openly proclaims the "right," hitherto left implicit, of the United States to dictate not merely the particular policies of other countries but their entire government and governing structure.

Military mercantilism: Roughly speaking, mercantilism is a policy designed to make a country's balance of payments or current account as positive as possible. It was practiced strenuously by the British Empire, which until World War I always ran a massive current account surplus. The United States has a gigantic and growing current account deficit. As mentioned earlier, this would normally exert a progressive weakening pressure on the currency, likely leading to a loss of economic prominence.

In part, the United States is using overtly mercantilist efforts to offset this possibility. The administration's levying of steel tariffs and its bloated farm subsidy bill were in part attempts to shore up a domestic vote base, but they were also a clear statement that the United States will not allow the strictures of the World Trade Organization to keep it from strong-arm moves to benefit U.S. corporations at the expense of others (although it will still, of course, use the WTO to stop other countries from similar efforts).

The primary way to prop up U.S. economic domination, however, is direct and indirect use of military power to gain an advantage. Thus, as opposed to "globalization" a la Clinton, we see wars that specifically benefit U.S. corporations at the expense of European ones, instead of policies, like creation of the WTO, roughly aimed at benefiting most First World corporations. Europe is on a rough economic par with the United States, yet politically it is nowhere in comparison. The agenda of the world is driven by the United States—we have a Washington consensus, not a Brussels consensus. This is true even with the economic liabilities being incurred by the United States' massive consumption. The distinction that allows the United States to maintain this pre-eminence is very clearly the political power that comes from military supremacy and a willingness to use it. The visible trend toward this line of thinking in the late Clinton years has exploded off the charts since 9/11.

Related to this is the undermining of multilateral financial institutions. Former Treasury Secretary Paul O'Neill did his best to undermine multilateral economic institutions like the World Bank and the IMF, most famously by quipping that Brazil should not be bailed out because the money would end in "Swiss bank accounts," a comment that caused the value of the real to crash, and also infuriated global bankers.[196] This has been accompanied by a turn to bilateral foreign aid, with a proposal to nearly double it by 2006.[197] As an instrument of economic and political leverage, bilateral aid can be wielded directly by the United States without concern for Germany, France, and Japan. The amount of money involved is again small, but the rhetorical challenge to the IMF and World Bank is great.

Convergence of Israeli and American "strategic interests" in the Middle East: One of the questions on everyone's lips is the role of Israel's supporters in shaping this new foreign policy. Undoubtedly, they are in the ascendant in the public eye; undoubtedly they have significant power on Capitol Hill and in the larger society, especially when combined with the Christian Right. They benefit also from a strong feeling of cultural affinity—Israel has always been represented since the early days of the Zionist movement as an outpost of Europe in the Middle East.

However, notwithstanding their considerable influence, it is equally certain that Israel supporters do not run things in Washington. It is the United States that is the superpower and it is an American elite that the government is attempting to serve. What is happening is that, with the fall of the Soviet Union, there is a greater and greater convergence between U.S. and Israeli "strategic interests." For the Sharonist wing in Israel, and the neoconservatives in the United States, the convergence is almost complete.

The reason is simple—in the calculations of the policymakers, the Arab states no longer have a choice. They can't go to the Soviet sphere; they certainly can't embark on an independent economic policy any more than any Third World country could by itself. When Israel invaded southern Lebanon in 1982, many U.S. policymakers were deeply concerned about the possibility that disaffected Arab states would deal more with the Soviet Union. Today, the United States can easily get away with more and more open support for the policies of a "Greater Israel"—and that is what is being done, notwithstanding the rhetorical support for a "Palestinian state."

Marriage of realpolitik and ideological visions: Richard Perle and Paul Wolfowitz are the ideological descendants (and former aides) of Washington senator Henry "Scoop" Jackson, the ultimate Cold War liberal; he made waves in the 1970s crusading against the oil companies because their callous regard for their own profits caused them to favor "abandoning" Israel. Perle and Wolfowitz are the forces behind the current policy, overseen by George W. Bush and Dick Cheney, the representatives of that same venal domestic oil industry. Colin Powell the "statesman" pushes through international "diplomacy" to advance the plans of the autocratic, imperial Donald Rumsfeld, who casually dismisses two of the most staunch allies of the United States as "old Europe." This marriage is possible because of unipolarity; it also makes the fanatic ideological side far more dangerous than it could have been otherwise.

THE LOSS OF IMPERIAL LEGITIMACY

Something else is new about this new imperialism as well. It is a very dark vision, even darker if possible than the Clintonite one that saw a world of increasing inequality, with the continent of Africa, much of south Asia, and rural China completely written off. It is also a vision that has lost all legitimacy not only with the people of the world but with many of the elite as well.

The protests of February 15, 2003, were something new

in the history of the world. In every country, there are people who follow U.S. policy, understand what it's about, and accept the importance of opposing it. The 11 million who marched against the war on Iraq were only part of a larger phenomenon. At Davos, at the World Economic Forum, according to an accidentally leaked e-mail from *Newsday* writer Laurie Garrett,[198] the mood was more anti-American than ever. On March 1, 2003, the Turkish parliament actually rejected a resolution allowing for Turkey to be used as a staging area for the war—even though the inducement was $15 billion in aid and grants and even in spite of the obvious risk of severe punishment from the IMF. France not only openly opposed the U.S. drive to war, it even did its own counter-"diplomacy," getting 52 African nations to agree to a declaration calling for more time.[199]

At a global AIDS conference in Barcelona, when U.S. Health Secretary Tommy Thompson was heckled by demonstrators, the audience cheered the hecklers. And the audience did not come from the slums of Manila or Calcutta—they were government officials and "important" NGO representatives. At the World Summit on Sustainable Development in Johannesburg, Colin Powell was booed.

The press is reporting that around the world George W. Bush is considered a far greater threat to world peace than Saddam Hussein or Kim Jong Il or whomever the United States targets tomorrow.

While the American empire has never ridden higher in

terms of absolute power, its base of acquiescence and support is getting weaker by the day. The dark vision can be opposed, and maybe even stopped.

THE SIREN SONG OF THE "DECENT LEFT"

At exactly the time of maximal ferment, both domestically and internationally, the antiwar movement in the United States was afflicted with a variety of self-appointed spokespeople who were very careful to tell us the right and wrong ways to oppose the war. For Todd Gitlin, Marc Cooper, Michael Walzer, Michael Berube, and others, it was right for us to oppose the war on Iraq because it was poorly thought out, because it was a "distraction" from the war on terrorism, and similar reasons; it was and is not all right to question the fundamental goodness of America's role in the world, it wasn't all right to oppose the war on Afghanistan, and it wasn't all right to oppose the sanctions on Iraq or to argue that Iraq posed no significant threat beyond its borders.

As Walzer wrote in the *New York Review of Books*, "Defending the embargo, the American overflights, and the U.N. inspections: This is the right way to oppose, and to avoid, a war."[200] That's the embargo that destroyed a society, the American overflights combined with bombing that were the prelude to a war, and the U.N. inspections that prepared the way for that war by disarming the targeted enemy.

Without delving too much into their tendentious reasoning, or into their total lack of contribution to any antiwar movement, their continuing role now is very clear. They were and are trying to keep the antiwar movement both from becoming a more sustained movement and from being an anti-imperialist movement, two considerations that are linked.

The dangers of this approach should by now be evident. The mainstream of the anti–Vietnam War movement was always actuated more by immediate concern with American casualties than with other important issues, and many continued to think of the Vietnam War as an aberration rather than an epitome of U.S. foreign policy. As a result, once U.S. troops withdrew in 1973, the movement largely disappeared even as the United States violated the Paris Peace Accords and continued to heavily arm South Vietnam. From 1975 to 1994, while Vietnam was subject to some of the most crippling sanctions ever levied by the United States (Iraq is Number One), while Vietnam was losing the "peace" and being slowly prepared for recolonization, there was hardly a peep out of the movement.

The anti–Gulf War movement, which was even more focused on potential American casualties and less prepared to deal with the realities of U.S. foreign policy, collapsed almost immediately. As a result, when the anti-Iraq-sanctions advocacy group, Voices in the Wilderness, formed in 1996, they truly were voices in the wilderness.

Few had paid any attention for five years while the people of Iraq suffered.

The war on Iraq was actively opposed around the world, not just because of the sympathy and solidarity people felt with the people of Iraq, but because people knew that the war was about more than Iraq. The war was a major step toward ushering in that dark vision mentioned earlier. In that vision, there is no law between nations, only the rule of force; there are no institutions with any legitimacy except the American military and the American corporation; the rising tide of economic inequality reaches cancerous proportions; the despolia-tion of the planet is accelerated beyond all reason for the most venal calculations of immediate gain; democracy is a shell game designed to fool the masses; the continent of Africa, except for the oil-bearing regions, is consigned to Outer Darkness; and all movements for global justice are crushed immediately into nonexistence.

The failure of the anti–Vietnam War movement to oppose Vietnam's slow strangulation through the ensuing "peace" was a real tragedy. It was avoidable had there been a better understanding of the situation—many did oppose the Vietnam War out of deeply held moral convictions and were repulsed by the vision of their country as, in the words of Dr. Martin Luther King, Jr., "the greatest purveyor of violence in the world today." Had that moral repulsion found a sustained, mass-based political avenue, the United States might have contributed something unique to the world's history: an empire brought down and transformed by the force of the moral vision of its citizens.

It still can.

Notes

1   "Russia Lawmakers Nix Erasing Iraq's Debt," Associated Press, April 11, 2003, www.guardian.co.uk/worldlatest/story/0,1280,-2552984,00.html.

2   "Pentagon Expects Long-Term Access to Four Key Bases in Iraq," Thom Shanker, Eric Schmitt, *New York Times*, April 20, 2003.

3   "Contracts to Rebuild Iraq Go to Chosen Few," Jackie Spinner, *Washington Post*, March 27, 2003; "Bechtel Wins Iraq Reconstruction Contract," Larry Margasak, Associated Press, April 17, 2003.

4   "Iraq 'May Have to Quit Opec'," Oliver Morgan, *The Observer*, April 27, 2003, www.guardian.co.uk/Iraq/Story/0,2763, 944126,00.html.

5   "National Energy Policy," Report of the National Energy Policy Development Group, May 2001, Ch. 8, p. 6, www.energy.gov/HQPress/releases01/maypr/national_energy_policy.pdf.

6   "The Man Who Would Be King of Iraq," Ian Williams, AlterNet, March 30, 2003, www.alternet.org/story.html?StoryID=15512.

7   "Iraqi Leaders Gather Under U.S. Tent: Government Planning Meeting Is Denounced as Unrepresentative by Uninvited," Keith B. Richburg, *Washington Post*, April 16, 2002.

8   "Iraqi Exile Criticizes Contract Awards," Reuters, April 19, 2003.

9   "More Die as Troops Open Fire on Mosul Crowd," Michael Howard, Rory McCarthy, *The Guardian*, April 17, 2003; "US Troops 'Kill 13 Iraqi Protesters'," Sarah Left, *The Guardian*, April 29, 2003; "U.S. Force Said to Kill 15 Iraqis During an Anti-American Rally," Ian Fisher, *New York Times*, April 30, 2003.

10 "U.S. Cuts Syria's Oil Lifeline," Paul Koring, *Toronto Globe and Mail*, April 16, 2003.

11 "Israeli Ambassador to US Calls for 'Regime Change' in Iran, Syria," Jonathan Wright, Reuters, April 28, 2003.

12 "U.S. Lawmakers Target Syria," Agence France Presse, April 10, 2003.

13 This process is analyzed in detail in "The Fateful Triangle," 2d ed., Noam Chomsky, 1999.

14 "UNRWA Launches $94 Million Appeal for West Bank and Gaza," UN Relief and Works Agency for Palestine Refugees in the Near East, December 10, 2002, at www.reliefweb.int.

15 The most illuminating source here is *Israel/Palestine: How to End the War of 1948,* Tanya Reinhart (New York: Seven Stories Press, 2002).

16 "Arafat Rejects Plan by Abu Mazen to Disarm Fatah Militia," Arnon Regular, *Ha'aretz*, April 23, 2003.

17 "PM: 'Iraq War Created an Opportunity with the Palestinians We Can't Miss'," Ari Shavit, *Ha'aretz*, April 21, 2003.

18 "U.S. to Press a Four-Step Plan for Transforming the Mideast," Robin Wright, *Los Angeles Times*, April 20, 2003.

19 "Thank God for the death of the UN: Its abject failure gave us only anarchy. The world needs order," Richard Perle, *The Guardian*, March 21, 2003, www.guardian.co.uk/comment/story/0,3604,918764,00.html.

20 "Bush Sees Aid Role of U.N. as Limited in Rebuilding Iraq," Richard W. Stevenson," *New York Times*, April 9, 2003.

21 "Annan Talks Up Postwar U.N. Role," John J. Goldman, Edwin Chen, *Los Angeles Times*, April 8, 2003.

22 "Germany May Help Iraq Reconstruction Even Without UN," Agence France Presse, April 7, 2003.

23 "France Urging U.N. to Suspend Iraq Penalties," Felicity Barringer, Elisabeth Bumiller, *New York Times*, April 23, 2003.

24 "U.S. Plans to Add to Teams to Hunt for Iraqi Weapons," Steven R. Weisman, *New York Times*, April 26, 2003.

25 *St. Petersburg Times*, November 1, 2001.

26 "Pakistan Halts Secret Plan for bin Laden Trial," Patrick Bishop, *Daily Telegraph*, October 4, 2001.

27 "U.S. Fumbles Chance to Nab Embassy Bombers: FBI Was Stopped From Pursuing East African Leads," by Michael Moran, reported July 30, 1999 on msnbc.com, still on the Web at http://ellen-bomer.com/Osama/Fumbles.html.

28 Op. cit.

29 "Qaeda's New Links Increase Threats From Far-Flung Sites," David Johnston, Don Van Natta Jr., and Judith Miller, *New York Times*, June 16, 2002.

30 "Combating Terrorism: Presidential Decision Directive 62," May 22, 1998, available at www.nbcindustrygroup.com/0522pres3.htm.

31 "Suspect Tells Police that Target of Bali Bombing was Americans, not Australians," Jane Perlez, *New York Times*, November 9, 2002, www.nytimes.com/2002/11/09/international/asia/09INDO.html.

32 "Bali Bomb Plotters Said to Plan to Hit Foreign Schools in Jakarta," Raymond Bonner with Jane Perlez, *New York Times*, November 18, 2002.

33 "CIA Told to Do 'Whatever Necessary' to Kill Bin Laden; Agency and Military Collaborating at 'Unprecedented' Level; Cheney Says War Against Terror 'May Never End,'" Bob Woodward, *Washington Post*, October 21, 2001.

34 From address to a joint session of Congress, September 20, 2001, www.whitehouse.gov/news/releases/2001/09/20010920-8.html.

35 Release date September 17, 2002. On the Web at www.whitehouse.gov/nsc/nss.html.

36 On the Web at www.newamericancentury.org/Rebuilding AmericasDefenses.pdf.

37 "Bush Planned Iraq 'Regime Change' Before Becoming President," Neil Mackay, *Scotland Sunday Herald*, Sept. 15, 2002, www.sundayherald.com/print27735.

38 NSS, Introduction.

39 Ibid., p. 29.

40 RAD, Introduction, p. i.

41 Ibid., p. 51.

42 Ibid., p. 18.

43 Ibid., p. 10

44 See, e.g., "The Rigged Missile Defense Test," Joe Conason, salon.com, July 31, 2001, http://archive.salon.com/news/col/cona/2001/07/31/test/.

45 RAD, p. 54.

46 Ibid., p. 53.

47 Ibid., p. 54.

48 Ibid., p. 4.

49 NSS, p. 15

50 Ibid., p. 31.
51 See, e.g., "Bush Administration Demands Immunity Agreement" by the Washington Working Group on the International Criminal Court, www.wfa.org/issues/wicc/article98/article98home.html, and "India-U.S. Deal to Boycott Court," December 26, 2002, http://news.bbc.co.uk/hi/south_asia/2606609.stm.
52 "On World Court, U.S. Focus Shifts to Shielding Officials," Elizabeth Becker, *New York Times*, September 7, 2002.
53 "Highlights of the FY04 Budget Request," Center for Defense Information, February 3, 2003, www.cdi.org/budget/2004. The number includes $379.9 billion for the Defense Department and $19.3 billion for the nuclear weapons functions of the Department of Energy.
54 "Nukes You Can Use," Stephen I. Schwartz, *Bulletin of the Atomic Scientists*, May/June 2002, Volume 58, No. 3, pp. 18-19, 69, www.thebulletin.org/issues/2002/mj02/mj02schwartz.html
55 "The Homegrown Nuclear Threat," Carrie Benzschawel, Common Dreams, Februrary 26, 2002, www.commondreams.org/views02/0226-07.htm.
56 "U.S. Air Bases Forge Double-Edged Sword," William M. Arkin, *Los Angeles Times*, January 6, 2002.
57 Op. cit.
58 "Operation Endless Deployment," William D. Hartung, Frida Berrigan, Michelle Ciarrocca, *The Nation*, October 21, 2002, www.commondreams.org/views02/1004-05.htm.
59 "Wider Military Ties With India Offer U.S. Diplomatic Leverage," Celia W. Dugger, *New York Times*, June 10, 2002.
60 "Philippine False Start For US Combatants," Mark Baker, *Sydney Morning Herald*, March 3, 2003; "U.S. Troops Arrive in Philippines for War Game," Reuters, April 17, 2003.
61 "Camp Bondsteel and America's Plans to Control Caspian oil," Paul Stuart, World Socialist Web Site, April 29, 2002, www.wsws.org/articles/2002/apr2002/oil-a29.shtml.
62 See, e.g., the Sunshine Project, www.sunshine-project.org
63 "New Role for U.S. in Colombia: Protecting a Vital Oil Pipeline," Juan Forero, *New York Times*, October 4, 2002.
64 "Bush Officials Met With Venezuelans Who Ousted Leader," Christopher Marquis, *New York Times*, April 16, 2002.

65 "U.S. Bankrolling Is Under Scrutiny for Ties to Chavez Ouster," Christopher Marquis, *New York Times*, April 25, 2002.

66 "Milosevic, Trailing in Polls, Rails Against NATO," Steven Erlanger, *New York Times*, September 20, 2000.

67 "Anatomy of a Coup," Conn Hallinan, *San Francisco Examiner*, May 3, 2002, available on the Web at www.globalresearch.ca/articles/HAL205A.html.

68 For commentary on the term, see my book *The New Crusade: America's War on Terrorism*, Section 2.

69 "Report on Humanitarian Needs in Iraq in the Immediate Post-Crisis Environment by a Mission to the Area Led by the Under-Secretary-General for Administration and Management," S/22366, March 20, 1991, on the Web at www.casi.org.uk/info/undocs/s22366.html.

70 *The Scourging of Iraq: Sanctions, Law and Natural Justice*, Geoff Simons (2d ed., New York: St. Martin's Press, 1998), p. 115.

71 "The March to War: From Day One to War's End and Beyond," James Ridgeway, ed. (New York: Four Walls, Eight Windows, 1991), p. 135.

72 The Desert Fox bombing campaign, carried out by U.S. and U.K. forces, involved more than 400 cruise missiles and numerous conventional bombs. It is covered in some detail later in this book.

73 S/1999/356, Celso Amorim, March 30,1999, on the Web at www.un.org/Depts/unmovic/documents/AMORIM.PDF

74 *War on Iraq: What Team Bush Doesn't Want you to Know*, William Rivers Pitt with Scott Ritter (New York: Context Books, 2002), p. 29.

75 "The Case for Iraq's Qualitative Disarmament," Scott Ritter, *Arms Control Today*, June 2000, www.armscontrol.org/act/2000_06/iraqjun.asp.

76 The Institute for Public Accuracy has a useful compilation of quotes at www.accuracy.org/iraq.

77 Warren Christopher, *New York Times*, April 29, 1994, cited in "Neighbors, Not Friends: Iraq and Iran After the Gulf Wars," Dilip Hiro (New York: Rutledge, 2001), p. 76.

78 *The Greatest Threat*, Richard Butler (New York: Public Affairs, 2000), p. 176.

79 Ibid., p. 185. This story is developed in more detail in *War Plan Iraq: Ten Reasons Against War on Iraq*, Milan Rai (London: Verso, 2002), pp. 47–54.

80 *Financial Times*, November 2, 1998, cited in Rai, p. 48.

81 Told in more detail in Rai, pp. 49-52.

82 Hiro, op. cit., p. 161.

83 "U.S. Says It Collected Iraq Intelligence Via UNSCOM," Thomas W. Lippman, Barton Gellman, *Washington Post*, January 8, 1999.

84 *The Threatening Storm: the Case for Invading Iraq*, Kenneth M. Pollack (New York: Random House, 2002), p. 93.

85 "Weapons Inspections Were 'Manipulated'," Carola Hoyos, Nick George, Roula Khalaf, *Financial Times*, July 29, 2002.

86 "A Smart Peace Movement Is MIA," Marc Cooper, *Los Angeles Times*, September 29, 2002.

87 For a fuller discussion of the problems of the South Africa analogy and of the sanctions paradigm, see my "Movement for Global Justice? The Fight over PNTR with China," www.zmag.org/globalchina.htm.

88 "Report on Humanitarian Needs in Iraq in the Immediate Post-Crisis Environment by a Mission to the Area Led by the Under-Secretary-General for Administration and Management, 10–17 March 1991," S/22366, March 20, 1991, www.un.org/Depts/oip/background/reports/s22366.pdf.

89 "Child Malnutrition Prevalent in Central/South Iraq," UNICEF, www.unicef.org/newsline/prgva11.htm.

90 Rai, op. cit., p. 178.

91 Available on the Web at www.unicef.org/reseval/iraqr.htm.

92 "Results of the 1999 Iraq Child and Maternal Mortality Surveys," www.unicef.org/reseval/iraqr.html Most of the field research was done by Iraqis, but UNICEF staff conducted elaborate statistical cross-checks to ensure that the data was not tainted.

93 "Sanctioning Saddam: The Politics of Intervention in Iraq," Sarah Graham-Brown (New York: I. B. Tauris, 1999), pp. 72-73.

94 Ibid., p. 75.

95 Special Report on FAO/WFP Food Supply and Nutrition Assessment Mission to Iraq, October 3, 1997, www.fao.org/WAICENT/faoinfo/economic/giews/english/alertes/srirq997.htm.

96 Graham-Brown, op. cit., p. 81.

97   Ibid., p. 72.

98   "Economic Sanctions as a Weapon of Mass Destruction," Joy Gordon, *Harper's* magazine, November 2002.

99   Ibid.

100 Ibid.

101 Ibid.

102 For a fuller description, see "The Secret Behind the Sanctions: How the US Intentionally Destroyed Iraq's Water Supply," Thomas Nagy, *The Progressive*, August 10, 2001.

103 Gordon, op. cit.

104 "In Search of an Iraqi Policy," Editorial, *The Economist*, February 24, 2001.

105 UN Secretary-General's Report, S/2001/186, March 5, 2001.

106 Human Rights Watch, August 2000, www.hrw.org/press/2000/08/iraq0804.htm.

107 UN Secretary-General's Report, S/2001/505, May 14, 2001, paragraph 29.

108 "Plans for Iraq Attack Began on 9/11," *CBS News*, September 4, 2002, www.cbsnews.com/stories/2002/09/04/september11/main520830.shtml.

109 See, e.g., "U.S. Inquiry Tried, but Failed, to Link Iraq to Anthrax Attack," William J. Broad and David Johnston, *New York Times*, December 22, 2001, www.commondreams.org/headlines01/1222-02.htm.
        "Anthrax Matches Army Spores—Bioterror: Organisms made at a military laboratory in Utah are genetically identical to those mailed to members of Congress," Scott Shane, *Baltimore Sun*, December 12, 2001, www.commondreams.org/headlines01/1212-01.htm.

110 "Bolton Says Iraq, North Korea Violate Biological Weapons Pact," U.S. State Department, sent on US-IRAQPOLICY list, November 19, 2001.

111 On MSNBC's *Hardball with Chris Matthews*, May 1, 2002.

112 "Preemptive Strike on Iraq to Improve Peace Prospects," Henry Kissinger, *Manila Times*, August 11, 2002, www.manilatimes.net/national/2002/aug/11/top_stories/20020811top6.html. A version of this piece was widely published, from the *Houston Chronicle* to the *Washington Post*.

113 "Go Slow on Iraq," Mark Dayton, *Washington Post*, September 29, 2002, www.washingtonpost.com/wp-dyn/articles/A13224-2002Sep27.html.

114 See, e.g., Quadrennial Defense Review Report, September 30, 2001.

115 "U.N. Official: Fake Iraq Nuke Papers Were Crude," Reuters, March 25, 2003.

116 "Blix Attacks 'Shaky' Intelligence on Weapons," Gary Younge, Richard Norton-Taylor, Patrick Wintour, *The Guardian*, April 23, 2003, www.guardian.co.uk/Iraq/Story/0,2763,941533,00.html.

117 "Exclusive: The Defector's Secrets," John Barry, *Newsweek*, March 3, 2003, www.msnbc.com/news/876128.asp?cp1=1. A transcript of the interview can be found at http://middleeastreference.org.uk/kamel.html.

118 "Inspectors Call U.S. Tips 'Garbage'," *CBS News*, February 20, 2003, www.cbsnews.com/stories/2003/01/18/iraq/main537096.shtml.

119 "U.S. Says Hussein Must Cede Power to Head Off War," Felicity Barringer with David E. Sanger, *New York Times*, March 1, 2003.

120 "Patterns of Global Terrorism 2000," U. S. State Department, in section called "Overview of State-sponsored Terrorism," www.state.gov/s/ct/rls/pgtrpt/2000/.

121 "A Case Not Closed," Seymour M. Hersh, *The New Yorker*, November 1, 1993, www.newyorker.com/archive/content/?020930fr_archive02.

122 "Calls for New Push Into Iraq Gain Power in Washington." Elaine Sciolino, Alison Mitchell, *New York Times*, December 3, 2001.

123 "Saad al-Bazzaz: An Insider's View of Iraq," *Middle East Quarterly*, December 1995, p. 69, cited in Pollack, p. 154.

124 Reported variously, including in "CIA Says Iraq Stopping Short of Terrorism vs U.S.," Tabassum Zakaria, Reuters, October 8, 2002, on the Web at www.philly.com/mld/philly/news/nation/4238650.htm.

125 "White House 'Exaggerating Iraqi threat:' Bush's televised address attacked by US intelligence," Julian Borger, *The Guardian*, October 9, 2002, www.guardian.co.uk/international/story/0,3604,807194,00.html.

126 *Spider's Web: The Secret History of How the White House Illegally Armed Iraq*, Alan Friedman (New York: Bantam Books, 1993), p. 104.

127 See, e.g., *The Longest War: The Iran-Iraq Military Conflict*, Dilip Hiro (New York: Routledge, 1991), and *The Culture of Terrorism*, Noam Chomsky (Boston: South End Press, 1988).

128 See, e.g., *Saddam Hussein: The Politics of Revenge*, Said K. Aburish (New York: Bloomsbury Publishing, 2000), pp. 249–250.

129 "America Didn't Seem to Mind Poison Gas," Joost R. Hilterman, *International Herald Tribune*, January 17, 2003, www.common-dreams.org/views03/0117-01.htm.

130 See *The March to War*, James Ridgway, ed. (New York: Four Walls, Eight Windows, 1991), p. 30; *Desert Shield to Desert Storm: The Second Gulf War*, Dilip Hiro (New York: Routledge, 1992), p. 94; *Iraq: From Sumer to Saddam*, Geoff Simons (New York: St. Martin's Press, 1994), p. 351.

131 *RN: The Memoirs of Richard Nixon*, Richard Nixon (New York: Warner Books, 1978), p. 490, cited in Rai, p. 194.

132 See, e.g., "Poll: No Rush To War," *CBS News* Poll, September 24, 2002, http://cbsnews.cbs.com/stories/2002/09/24/opinion/polls/main523130.shtml.

133 "Apparatus of Lies: Saddam's Disinformation and Propaganda 1990-2003," White House document, www.whitehouse.gov/ogc/apparatus.

134 "Purported bin Laden Message on War Against Infidels," CNN, February 11, 2003, www.cnn.com/2003/WORLD/meast/02/11/binladen.excerpts/index.html. Numerous transcripts are available and will have slightly different translation.

135 "Prague Discounts an Iraqi Meeting," James Risen, *New York Times*, October 21, 2002.

136 "Bin Laden-Iraq Link Suddenly Emerges," Mark Mackinnon, Alan Freeman, *Toronto Globe and Mail*, February 6, 2003.

137 "Exiled Mullah Denies Claims of Terror Ties Made by U.S.," Don Van Natta Jr., *New York Times*, February 6, 2003.

138 "Terrorism Experts Doubt bin Laden, Baghdad Link," Timothy Appleby with files from Alan Freeman, *Toronto Globe and Mail*, February 6, 2003.

139 "Dubious Iraqi Link," David Ignatius, *Washington Post*, March 14, 2002.

140 "Allies Find No Links Between Iraq, Al Qaeda," Sebastian Rotella, *Los Angeles Times*, November 4, 2002.

141 Senate Foreign Relations Committee Testimony, July 31, 2002.

142 "Beyond Bali: ASPI's Strategic Assessment 2002," Australian Strategic Policy Institute, www.aspi.org.au/beyondbali/.

143 "IAEA Update Report to the Security Council Pursuant to Resolution 1441," Mohammed el-Baradei, January 27, 2003, www.iaea.org/worldatom/Press/Focus/IaeaIraq/unscre-port_290103.html.

144 "Chemical Coup d'Etat," George Monbiot, *The Guardian*, April 16, 2002; "Diplomacy US-Style," George Monbiot, *The Guardian*, April 23, 2002.

145 "U.S. Tells Iran, Syria, North Korea: Learn from Iraq," Philip Pullella, Reuters, April 9, 2003.

146 "North Korea Says Its Arms Will Deter U.S. Attack," Howard W. French, *New York Times*, April 7, 2003.

147 "Korean Diplomacy Enters a New Era," Howard W. French, *New York Times*, April 20, 2003.

148 "United Nations Security Council Resolutions Currently Being Violated by Countries Other than Iraq," Stephen Zunes, *Foreign Policy in Focus Commentary*, February 28, 2003, www.fpif.org/commentary/2002/0210unres.html.

149 "Rumsfeld Adds Targets in 'No Fly' Enforcement," Robert Schlesinger, *Boston Globe* September 17, 2002.

150 "Britain and US Step up Bombing in Iraq: Ministry of Defence reveals 300 percent rise in ordnance dropped over southern no-fly zone," Richard Norton-Taylor, *The Guardian*, December 4, 2002, www.guardian.co.uk/international/story/0,3604,853260,00.html.

151 The Colorado Campaign for Middle East Peace keeps a record of wire reports of all bombings at www.ccmep.org/usbombing-watch/2003.htm.

152 Covered at greater length in my *The New Crusade: America's War on Terrorism*, pp. 112–113.

153 Op. cit., pp. 28-29.

154 "Pentagon Planning, Not Diplomacy, Sets U.S. Agenda on Iraq," Michael T. Klare, *Foreign Policy in Focus*, February 17, 2003, www.presentdanger.org/commentary/2003/0302milplan.html.

155 See, e.g., "U.S. Plan for Iraq Is Said to Include Attack on 3 Sides," Eric Schmitt, *New York Times*, July 5, 2002; "How to Paint a

Bullseye on Iraq," Ron Brackett, *St. Petersburg Times*, August 18, 2002.

156 Klare, op. cit.

157 "U.S. Plan for Saddam: Shock and Awe William Bunch, *Philadelphia Daily News*, February 26, 2003. "Analysis: Strategic bombing in Iraq war," Thomas Houlahan, United Press International, April 23, 2002, www.upi.com/view.cfm?StoryID=20030423-040349-4735r.

158 See, e.g., "Bechtel Strikes Back at Bolivia," Jim Shultz, Pacific News Service, Alternet, November 11, 2002, www.alternet.org/story.html?StoryID=14525.

159 "US Holds Out at WTO Talks on Medicines, Access," Agence France-Presse, December 16, 2002, www.aegis.com/news/afp/2002/AF0212C1.html.

160 Section 2, "The New White Man's Burden," in *The New Crusade*, pp. 99–123.

161 *Out of the Ashes: the Resurrection of Saddam Hussein*, Andrew and Patrick Cockburn, New York: HarperCollins 1999, p. 74.

162 *Saddam Hussein: The Politics of Revenge*, Said K. Aburish, London: Bloomsbury 2000, p. 308.

163 Op. cit. 310. The suppression of the uprising is discussed at more length in *War Plan Iraq: Ten Reasons Against War on Iraq*, Milan Rai (London: Verso, 2002), pp. 75-83.

164 Hiro, pp. 36-37.

165 "A Rising Sense That Iraq's Hussein Must Go," Thomas L. Friedman, *New York Times*, July 7, 1991.

166 "The Warlords Win in Kabul," Omar Zakhilwal, Adeena Niazi, *New York Times*, June 21, 2002.

167 "US pulls out Karzai's military bodyguards," Peter Beaumont, *The Observer*, Sunday November 24, 2002, www.observer.co.uk/afghanistan/story/0,1501,846595,00.html

168 "Abrupt Amnesty At Iraqi Prisons: A Joy for Many, Grief for Some," John F. Burns, *New York Times*, October 22, 2002.

169 "Political Detainees Still Held; Prison Papers Forged," Iraq Press, Arbil (northern Iraq), December 18, 2002, www.iraqpress.org/english.asp?fname=ipenglish\00olde\9999ehum72.htm.

170 "Brits Fighting Fierce Battles With 1000 Militia Near Basra," D. Melgren, C. Hanley, Associated Press, March 26, 2003.

171 "Basra Now Military Target, Says UK," CNN, March 25, 2003, www.cnn.com/2003/WORLD/europe/03/25/sprj.irq.basra/index. html.

172 "Food For Southern Iraq Pre-positioned in the Region, Says Natsios," USAID Press briefing, March 25, 2003.

173 "Grisly Results of U.S. Cluster Bombs," Thomas Frank, *Newsday*, April 15, 2003, www.newsday.com/news/nation-world/iraq/ny-woclus0415.story.

174 "Good Kills," Peter Maass, *The New York Times Magazine*, April 20, 2003.

175 See *The Prize: the Epic Quest for Oil, Money, and Power*, Daniel Yergin (New York: Touchstone, 1992), for an exhaustive reference on oil-related issues.

176 Official US State Department history 1945, Volume 8, p. 45.

177 Op. cit., pp. 535-7.

178 Op. cit., p. 757.

179 "With War, Africa Oil Beckons," Ken Silverstein, *Los Angeles Times*, March 21, 2003.

180 "Iraq Country Analysis Brief," U.S. Energy Information Administration, February 2003, www.eia.doe.gov/emeu/cabs/iraq.html.

181 "Repatriating Migrant Arab Capital? Say 'Inshallah,'" *Lebanon Daily Star*, December 30, 2002.

182 "Firm's Iraq Deals Greater Than Cheney Has Said," Colum Lynch, *Washington Post*, June 21, 2001.

183 "Iraq Country Analysis Brief," U.S. Energy Information Administration, February 2003, www.eia.doe.gov/emeu/cabs/iraq.html.

184 "Oil Firms Wait as Iraq Crisis Unfolds," Robert Collier, *San Francisco Chronicle*, September 29, 2002.

185 "In Iraqi War Scenario, Oil Is Key Issue: U.S. Drillers Eye Huge Petroleum Pool," Dan Morgan, David B. Ottaway, *Washington Post*, September 15, 2002, www.washingtonpost.com/ac2/wp-dyn/A18841-2002Sep14.

186 "BP Chief Fears US Will Carve up Iraqi Oil Riches," Terry MacAlister, *The Guardian*, October 30, 2002, www.guardian.co.uk/oil/story/0,11319,822229,00.html.

187 "Saudis to Boost Oil Output in Case of Iraq War-US," Reuters, February 26, 2002.

188 "In Quietly Courting Africa, U.S. Likes the Dowry: Oil," James Dao, *New York Times*, September 19, 2002.

189 "Slump Aside, Trade Deficit Hits a Record," David Leonhardt, *New York Times*, February 21, 2003.

190 See "Behind the Invasion of Iraq," Research Unit for Political Economy, December 2002, www.rupe-india.org/34/behind.html, for further discussion of this point.

191 "The Battle for Energy Dominance," Edward Morse, James Richard, *Foreign Affairs*, March/April 2002, p. 23.

192 "Saudi Arabia Withdraws Natural Gas Deal," September 09, 2002, Rigzone.com, www.rigzone.com/news/article.asp?a_id=4257.

193 "The President's Real Goal in Iraq," Jay Bookman, *Atlanta Journal-Constitution*, September 29, 2002, www.accessatlanta.com/ajc/opinion/0902/29bookman.html.

194 For a discussion, see my *The New Crusade*, Section 2, "The New White Man's Burden."

195 "Review of Current Trends: U.S. Foreign Policy," PPS 23, George Kennan, February 24, 1948. Excerpts in *Containment: Documents on American Policy and Strategy, 1945–1950*, Thomas H. Etzold, John Lewis Gadds, eds. (New York: Columbia University Press, 1978).

196 "Bush's Lost Continent: The President Promised South America Close Friendship, No Bailouts. Why He Switched on Both," CNN, August 12, 2002, www.cnn.com/2002/ALLPOLITICS/08/12/time.bush.

197 "After Bush Push on Foreign Aid: Getting Results," David R. Francis, *Christian Science Monitor*, April 01, 2002, www.csmonitor.com/2002/0401/p21s01-wmgn.html.

198 This email was widely circulated on the Internet. Ms. Garrett has acknowledged it as her own. It is posted at www.topica.com/lists/psychohistory/read/message.html?sort=d&mid=1711891071&start=4389.

199 "52 African Countries Endorse French Opposition to War on Iraq," Glenn Frankel, *Washington Post*, February 22, 2003.

200 "The Right Way," Michael Walzer, *The New York Review of Books*, March 13, 2003, www.nybooks.com/articles/16110.

About the Author

RAHUL MAHAJAN (Ph.D. University of Texas at Austin) is a longtime antiwar activist at the local and national level. He is a founding member of the Nowar Collective (www.nowarcollective.com) and serves on the National Board of Peace Action, the nation's largest grassroots peace organization. His first book, *The New Crusade: America's War on Terrorism*, has been described as "mandatory reading for all those who want to get a handle on the war on terrorism." He writes frequently for mainstream and alternative print media and for websites like Common Dreams, Zmag.org, Alternet, and Counterpunch. His writing can be found at www.rahul-mahajan.com. He can be reached at rahul@tao.ca.